# TRANSNATIONAL BUSINESS AND CORPORATE CULTURE

## Problems and Opportunities

*edited by*

STUART BRUCHEY
Allan Nevins Professor Emeritus
Columbia University

# GLOBALIZATION OF SMALL ECONOMIES AS A STRATEGIC BEHAVIOR IN INTERNATIONAL BUSINESS

SERGIO A. CASTELLO
TERUTOMO OZAWA

Routledge
Taylor & Francis Group
LONDON AND NEW YORK

Published 1999 by Routledge
2 Park Square, Milton Park, Abingdon, Oxfordshire OX14 4RN
711 Third Avenue, New York, NY 10017

First issued in paperback 2016

*Routledge is an imprint of the Taylor and Francis Group, an informa business*



Library of Congress Cataloging-in-Publication Data
Castello, Sergio A., 1966–
Globalization of small economies as a strategic behavior in international business / Sergio A. Castello, Terutomo Ozawa.
p. cm. — (Transnational business and corporate culture)
Includes bibliographical references and index.
ISBN 0-8153-3307-2 (alk. paper)
1. Export marketing—Case studies. 2. Strategic planning—Case studies. 3. States, Small—Economic conditions—Case studies. 4. Competition, International—Case studies. I. Ozawa, Terutomo. II. Title. II. Series.
HF1416.C37 1999
382'.6—dc21 99-30105

ISBN 13: 978-1-138-97528-6 (pbk)
ISBN 13: 978-0-8153-3307-4 (hbk)

Publisher's Note
The publisher has gone to great lengths to ensure the quality of this reprint but points out that some imperfections in the original may be apparent.

# Contents

# Tables

# Figures

# Preface

The number of nations has doubled in the last half a century to around 200 independent economic units. Moreover, the break-up of the Soviet bloc into a large number of small independent nations in Central and Eastern Europe and the continued threat of separatist groups (i. e. Canada, Spain, and Sri Lanka) have sparked economists' interest to focus on the size of nations once again. This study offers a more comprehensive measurement of smallness than the conventional one for the analysis of the globalization strategies and structural adaptability of countries to overcome smallness within the context of the European Union and two case studies (i. e. Catalonia and New Zealand). The central issue involved in this book is whether small independent economic units can survive and prosper with their own limited domestic market.

To address this matter, this study postulates the propositions that small economies exhibit a higher degree of outward orientation and structural adaptability, compared to their larger counterparts.

Small economies, when economically successful and compared to their larger counterparts, tend to be: more export focused in manufacturing, likely to specialize in differentiated manufactures, more actively involved with direct overseas businesses, more sensitive in strategically managing exchange rates, likely to be in a better position to achieve price stability, more actively involved in international trade through varying degrees of economic integration, likely to have a higher degree of flexibility, more actively involved to forge a complementary government/firm relationship, and likely to have a higher degree of corporatism.

The two main hypothesis of this book are empirically tested within the 1973–1992 period for the European Union and the 1985–1992 period for New Zealand. The importance of nation size, outward orientation, and structural adaptability is demonstrated in the estimated regressions, which showed significant results in the relations among smallness, globalization, and flexibility for the time periods studied.

This all points to the importance of developing specific approaches to outward orientation and structural adaptability to overcome smallness as the global economy continues to grow while the size of the parts continues to shrink.

# Acknowledgments

I would like to express my gratitude to Dr. Ozawa, who has given me continual support and inspiration in my research.

I would also like to express my thanks to my wife, Lora, and my five children, Katie, Kerri, Walker, Monica, and Sofia, who have been very supportive and understanding. Finally, thanks again, Lora, for all the much needed support.

# Globalization of Small Economies as a Strategic Behavior in International Business

CHAPTER 1

# Introduction

Literature on the economic implications of the size of nations is scarce. There are no macro-economic textbooks dealing with the theoretical implications of differences in size between various economies. This lack of interest in the subject has been perhaps caused by the leading position of American textbooks in this field. European economists usually show much greater interest in this topic[1]. American economists normally are not confronted with the constraints faced by small economies in this new era of economic globalization. It is a well established fact that in small economies the importance of trade is overwhelming, yet many economists either neglect trade or treat it as secondary factor, since they are mainly concerned with a "closed economy" model.

Thus it is not surprising that economists dealing with the subject of smallness do not share a standard definition of what it means. Some authors regard Canada and Australia as small nations and of course anything can be small relative to planet Earth. But it is hardly likely that restrictions of scale relevant to Malta have the same relevance to Luxembourg or Iceland, even though all three have less than half a million people. It seems that the meaning of smallness needs further research to establish common grounds for more fruitful debates on the implications of smallness and economic development. By and large, this is usually done by the size of the population. Other factors have been suggested, for example, total land surface, land area weighted for economic potential, the size of GNP, energy consumption or self-perception.

The concept of smallness is well worth pursuing especially in its relative sense within the context of economic development. Likewise, it is all the more relevant as the number of countries breaking up into smaller units continues to increase. Becker (1994, p. 20) writes: "The number of nations has almost doubled in the past 50 years, to 191 independent states. The economic cost of independence has been sharply lowered by the rapid growth in post-World War II of international trade." Thus, it is necessary to better understand their opportunities in this new global economic environment.

Moreover, the break up of the Soviet Union and the emergence of CIS (Commonwealth of Independent States), the break up of Czechoslovakia and the emergence of the Czech and Slovak states, and the break up of Yugoslavia and the emergence of who knows what should spark economists' interest to focus on the size of nations once again.

Naisbitt (1994) notes that Freddie Heineken, the brewer master in Holland, has proposed an alliance of Europe with 75 nations, each with a population of five to 10 million. Each nation would be small enough to have efficient and manageable institutions with reference to its cultural, religious, habits, and linguistic tradition. He writes: "Iceland, Norway, Sweden, Finland, and Denmark would stay the same. Scotland and Wales would become independent countries. In Spain, Catalonia and the Basque region would become independent. Paris and the area around it would become Ile-de-France, with a population of about 10 million. Switzerland and Italy would be divided into nine different countries. And so on." (Naisbitt 1994, p. 10).

Furthermore, the growth of international trade keeps binding nations, but it is also increasing the force of separatism. The more international trade and technology transfer bring nations together, the more uninhibited the moves to break nations apart. The growth of this type of global economy and the existence of ever-more powerful transnational corporations are creating a resurgence of nationalism. There are many regions of the world trying to accelerate the process of independence such as: Quebec in Canada, Tamil in Sri Lanka, Catalonia in Spain, the three regions of Wallonia, Flanders, and Brussels in Belgium, and finally the coastal province of Guangdong in China[2]. Thus, the relationship between institutions, political systems, and economic activities needs special attention in this new era of increasing nationalism forces around the world. In addition, a question is now raised, for example, about the economic viability and welfare implications of newly formed small nations[3].

Alesina and Spolaore (1995, p. 1) advocate the fact that national borders have been redrawn to an extent which is rather exceptional for modern times. They write: "These changes have been so remarkable that some observers begin to wonder whether the current nation states in Europe are becoming obsolete, threatened by regional movements from below and supernational economic integration from above."

Naisbitt (1994, p. 11) says: "The world's trends point overwhelmingly toward political independence and self-rule in one hand, and the formation of economic alliances on the other." Also, he puts forth the paradox that the bigger the world economy, the more powerful its smallest nations. As the world integrates economically, larger nations will become divided in smaller nations with more power and importance. Thus, the economic globalization of the world is growing while the size of the nations are shrinking.

Chapter Two is composed of the literature review on smallness, the salient characteristics of small nations, and a definition of small open economies. The concept of smallness will be defined based on a more dynamic, structuralism-based, and inductive reasoning approach. Also, the advantages and disadvantages of small countries will be described. Furthermore, an unconventional view of smallness will be presented. For purposes of this study, smallness will be defined as follows:

> "A compactedness of a nation in the domestic economic space with the attributes of a small population, a small geographical area, and a small area of natural resources." (Castello and Ozawa 1994).

Chapter Three looks at the globalization strategies and institutional flexibility of small open economies. The first part of the chapter is committed to the specific approaches of globalization to overcome smallness and to secure economic growth, with special attention to the two main engines of growth for small economies such as exports (through international trade) and FDI (through direct overseas business). Thus, small open economies tend to be: (1) more export focused in manufacturing, (2) likely to specialize in differentiated manufactures as they advance in industrialization, (3) more actively involved in direct overseas investment, (4) more sensitive in strategically managing exchange rates, (5) likely to be in a better position to achieve price stability, and (6) more actively involved in international trade through varying degrees of economic integration, than their larger counterparts.

The latter part of the chapter examines the institutional flexibility necessary for small nations to overcome smallness and to secure economic growth. Thus, small open economies tend to exhibit: (1) greater flexibility, (2) more effectiveness in macro-organizational strategies, and (3) a higher degree of corporatism, than their larger counterparts. Based on this analysis, some basic will be extracted and later tested in Chapter Four.

Chapter Four provides a classification, degree of globalization, and empirical evidence on the European Union, since it will be the focus of this study. Hence, it will include the results of the empirical testing of the propositions presented in Chapter Three.

Chapter Five looks at two region/country case studies. The region case is on Catalonia in Spain, and the country case is on New Zealand. Both Catalonia and New Zealand fall into the definition of small open economies. And Chapter Six gives the concluding remarks of the study and provides some economic direction for the newly industrializing small nations, and the newly formed independent states.

CHAPTER 2

# Literature Review of Smallness

## A Search for Salient Characteristics and a Definition

Many definitions have been used to determine the size of nations. Thus, it is not surprising that economists dealing with the subject of smallness do not have a conventional definition of what it means. Indeed, economists began to direct attention to the size of nations only in the wake of decolonization in the post-World-War II period.

Thus this chapter will be divided as follows: Section 2.1 will review the literature on the notion and definition of small open economies beginning in the 1950's until today. This section reveals the lack of consensus when determining the size of a nation, and the need for further research in this area. Section 2.2 will identify the salient economic characteristics of small economies.

Section 2.3 will present an unconventional view of smallness, as well as the proposition that small nations exhibit a higher degree of globalization than their larger counterparts. Finally, a summary will conclude the chapter.

### 2.1 LITERATURE REVIEW ON SMALLNESS

One of the few economists who have intensively studied the scale problems on an aggregate level is Kohr. In this field he ranks as a pioneer, though he is not clear neither on defining smallness nor on suggesting the optimal size of an economy. Kohr's contribution can be considered as a continuation of the utopian tradition in which the world should organize in tiny societies. For example, he considers that the economic optimum social size requires between 7,000 and 12,000 inhabitants (a figure existing in flourishing Andorra, Monaco, San

Marino, or Liechtenstein at that time). In the end, in order to fulfil the economic, political, and cultural functions a society should be sufficient between 100,000 and 200,000 members, although he allows the economic optimum social size to be expanded to perhaps 15 million under certain conditions (Kohr 1977, p. 17).

Indeed, economists began to direct more attention to the size of nations in the wake of decolonization in the post World War II period; in 1957 the International Economic Association held a conference on the "Economic Consequences of the Size of Nations" in Lisbon (Robinson 1960). Among other well known participants were Fabricant, Kuznets, and Scitovsky (Butter 1985, p. 22). Kuznets analyzed the 80 states which were independent in 1952, of which 47, with populations of less than 10 million, were considered small. Kuznets (1960) argued that the economic structure of small nations was so different from that of large nations that both could not be treated as comparable units in economic development.

Furthermore, the Commonwealth Studies of the University of London held a two year seminar on the problems of very small nations in 1962, with the resulting publication by B. Benedict (1967). Unfortunately, the papers were rather general dealing primarily with sociological, demographic, administrative, and political issues (Butter 1985, p.23).

Demas (1965) dealt with the economics of development in small countries with special reference to the Caribbean nations. He defined a small nation as one with population of 5 million and usable land area of 10 to 20 thousand square miles. Chenery and Taylor (1968) made comparisons concerning the size of nations for the post World War II period using statistical techniques in which 35 small nations were identified. They defined a small country one with a population of 15 million or less.

Thomas (1974), following Kohr's approach, wrote about the strategies of small dependent economies advocating for vertical integration of demand structure with domestic resource use in industry (p. 96). Thomas' approach cannot be considered as having too much practical application to the situation of small states. Late in the 1970's, the University of Amsterdam established a Small Economics Research Center with A.J. Butter as the Research Director. Butter published a book in 1985 on the subject criticizing the lack of literature and interest in the subject matter.

Dervis, de Melo, and Robinson (1982) following Chenery's approach, wrote about the general equilibrium models for development policy emphasizing the degree of openness of the economy as an important source of the variation of the pattern of growth. They did not focus on country size to determine the smallness of the nation, but they did specify that a small nation was one with a total labor force of 10 million. Also, Jalan (1982) defined a small nation as one with a population of 5 million with arable land of 25,000 sq. km., and a GNP of $2 billion.

Gayle (1986) wrote about the small developing state in reference to Costa Rica, Singapore, and Jamaica. He defined a small developing state as one with no less than 60,000 and not greater than 8 million people, a GNP per capita within the range of $1,000 and $7,000, and an area neither less than 234 sq. km. nor larger than 285,000 sq. km.

In 1987, the Institute of Production at Aalborg University Center organized an international seminar at Tannishus in Northern Denmark. The major theme discussed was the problems of small countries in confronting the rapid changes in technology which are transforming the structure of the world economy. They did not attempt to define smallness. The papers are oriented toward the problems of small economies in the sector of microelectronics and related information technologies.

Kaminarides, Briguglio, and Hoogendonk (1989) published a book with a collection of papers presented at the International Conference on the Economic Development of Small Countries held in Malta in 1985. They did not attempt to define smallness, instead they made some revealing observations on the breakdown of nations.

"There are 130 countries/territories or 70 percent of all countries/territories that have populations less than 10 million. There are 57 countries or 30 percent of all countries with population over 10 million." ". . . the 130 countries share only 7.6 percent of the total world population." (p. XV). Thus, they raise the question whether the economic literature will continue addressing the problems of the majority people living on fewer large countries or the problem concerning a large number of small countries in which less than 8 percent of the world population lives.

The authors made an important point about the criteria used to define small countries, since the groupings of these nations show a large number of characteristics. For example, if we take into account nations with a population of 200,000 to 500,000 inhabitants.

Luxembourg, Iceland, Malta, Barbados, and the Bahamas are included. However, these countries are experiencing different climates, physical and human resources, welfare levels, political, social, and cultural characteristics.

The World Development Journal in 1993 printed a collection of articles presented during an international conference on small states held in Valletta, Malta in 1991. The issue contains 13 articles dealing with small economies in a global or regional setting and country-specific studies.

Finally, Development and International Cooperation in 1997 printed another collection containing 14 articles dealing with the economic performance, characteristics, and opportunities of small countries, as well as several case studies of European economies.

Opinions have been expressed that the cut-off point around 1 million or less in population would exhibit a much more realistic picture for the topic of small nations and states. Harris (1970), UNITAR (1971), UNCTAD (1974), Plischke (1977), Dolman (1982), and Doumenge (1983), all advocate lower cut-off points. This book would be dealing then with micro-states and small islands, which is not its intention.

## 2.2 COMMON CHARACTERISTICS OF SMALL ECONOMIES

Small nations do not necessarily stand out for their unfavorable position in per capita income. However, even with high levels of per capita income, small countries tend to remain weak in terms of total economic size as well as bargaining power. Also, they are quite vulnerable to external shocks and cyclical fluctuations in the world economy since they are extremely dependent on international trade and their openness.

Small open economies are fairly diverse in economic characteristics. There are wide variations in their income per capita, population, land area, land-locked natural resources, and population density. But a common feature of small economies is their *openness*. Limited domestic market opportunities and usually a narrow natural resource base have encouraged firms of these economies to expand their markets through international trade. This openness is characterized by product and market concentration. These concentrations are obviously due to the narrow natural resource base and the need for specialization to secure scale economies not only in production but also in marketing, transportation, and distribution (Persaud 1989, p. 16).

There are many other common features among small nations, but in order to single out their salient characteristics, first it is necessary to examine the disadvantages and advantages of these small open economies.

### 2.2.1 Disadvantages of Small Nations

It is shown that small economies by their very nature tend to be less diversified and to have relatively high foreign trade risks. Some of the disadvantages of a small nation are:

1. The economic structure is less diversified than that of a large country at the same level of development because of the smaller domestic market, (there are exceptions like Finland, Sweden, and New Zealand).
2. The absolute size of its labor force does restrict the scope for differentiation within the labor market. The smaller a national labor market, the higher are the frictions caused by segmentation slowing the expansion of trades and professions. Labor then becomes a bottleneck and restricts the goods that can be produced at home.
3. As previously stated, international trade for a small nation is vital, and it becomes indispensable for its economic development. Large countries such as Brazil or Indonesia can develop without trade but Portugal and Greece are heavily dependent on trade to become fully developed. Furthermore, Belgium and Luxembourg could have not reached their developed nation status without international trade.
4. A small area diminishes the transport cost advantage of domestic suppliers. But for large nations, transport costs are a form of *natural* protection of home industries from import competition. A small country enjoys less of this kind of natural protection; therefore, it is more open to sometimes fierce import competition from abroad.
5. A small nation tends to be more heavily dependent on foreign sources of supply and on foreign markets. Also, its foreign trade is inevitably less diversified geographically than the one of a larger nation. Thus, exports in particular are more concentrated on the markets of a few countries such as Austria on Germany, and Ireland on Great Britain.

6. A small area, especially if it is land-locked, means less diversity in raw materials and natural resources. Obviously, there are exceptions such as Finland, Sweden, and New Zealand.
7. The defense burden for a small nation tends to be larger than for a larger counterpart, since it is a function of the size of the potential enemy. Costa Rica is the only small country that has abolished its army with very favorable effects on its social services. Moreover, the so-called 'Nordic' or 'Scandinavian' states have also seen favorable effects of their military neutrality.
8. Small manpower resources due to small population causes oftentimes shortages of skilled labor and training facilities, which are much needed for creation of knowledge to obtain dynamic comparative advantages.
9. A small economy attempts, indeed is forced, to extend its limited resources and to lower per capita costs by requiring senior officials to act in multi-functional roles.
10. Greater openness means less independence for a smaller economy in setting its macroeconomic policies, thus it is more at mercy of external shocks and of bigger countries' policies. For example, small European countries are at the mercy of Germany's monetary policies.

### 2.2.2 Advantages of Small Countries

Streeten (1993) points out that the differences in growth by region are much greater than those by size with East Asia at the top and Africa at the bottom. We find some spectacular success stories around the world, especially in East Asia, such as Hong Kong and Singapore. In addition, in the old continent of Europe, especially in Western Europe, great success stories can be found in Malta, Cyprus, Portugal, and Greece.

During 1960 to 1988, Malta's GDP growth has increased at a spectacular rate of 6.2% per year—Malta is in line as a candidate for membership to the EU. Moreover, Portugal's and Greece's GDP growth rates have been 4.4% and 4.2% respectively for the same period from 1960 to 1988 (Summers and Heston 1988, p. 358).

Some of the advantages of a small nation are:

1. For a small nation like Malta, rapid growth is due to the smallness of a rural hinterland, of the slow-coach agriculture. Urban industry can grow much faster than agriculture.
2. The ratio of foreign trade to national income is larger in a small economy such as Portugal or Greece than in a larger counterpart; therefore, they can create jobs for the rapidly growing labor force by concentrating on labor-intensive exports[4].
3. Progress means change, and change is bound to harm special groups. These groups do attempt to resist change, but in a small economy is likely to be less, and the harm more accepted or more compensated[5]. For example, Austria's corporate Keynesianism makes it possible to accept measures that would be more intensely resisted in a larger country, where the leaders of the groups (employers, farmers, trade union representatives, and politicians) do not know each other as well as in a small nation.
4. Adjustments to uncertainties and external shocks are more accepted if solidarity prevails. Moreover, a small nation is extremely *adaptable* and *flexible* to new challenges. In addition, Olson (1982) argues that external shocks are actually beneficial to economies as a Schumpeterian mechanism of "creative destruction" at the macroeconomic level[6].
5. A small nation tends to do a good job of educating its people with the exception of Portugal and Greece. Education is without a doubt an important wealth-sharing opportunity-creating mechanism. It creates opportunities for upward mobility facilitating the acceptance of new economic reforms. For example, in Ireland, Denmark, Finland, Sweden, Belgium, and Luxembourg it is very easy to contract skilled labor.
6. Adaptability achieved by producing for markets with high and rising demand means a constant reallocation of resources and a high rate of product innovation, which facilitates the creation of highly sophisticated companies—multinationals, which enhance international competitiveness. For example, Denmark, the Netherlands, Finland, and Sweden have all created their own successful multinationals.
7. A small state tends to develop a closely integrated society containing an intricate network of personal relationships due to shorter geographical distances and more frequent face-to-face

contacts, thus providing a high degree of interpersonal communication and an efficient flow of information among government and industry, which subsequently brings about the sound ties necessary for a complementary relationship between the two sectors. For example, New Zealand, Denmark, Portugal, Austria, and Sweden.

8. According to Johnson (1988, p. 295), a small number of important decision-makers operating in an environment of high cultural homogeneity and strong social cohesion puts forth a transparent society where the "rules of the game" are known by the economic agents. As Becker (1994) supports: "Because small economies are more homogeneous, they tend to suffer less from internal clashes among special interests" (p. 20). Moreover, it also means that government has a clear idea of what economic policy tools are accepted by the citizens. Furthermore, Alesina and Spolaore (1995, p. 4) write that in small countries the choices of the public are closer to the preferences of the average citizen than in larger countries. For example, Denmark, Austria, the Netherlands, and Sweden.
9. This capacity to generate compromises and reach consensus between opposing groups is *vital* for the high degree of corporatism that small economies exhibit. For example, the 'Nordic' countries, Austria, and the Netherlands enjoy a strong element of class compromise, parliamentary alliances and consensus seeking, thus making for quick responses to external challenges[7]. Moreover, this may imply that it is easier to achieve coherence and flexibility in the institutional system of small nations.

Based upon the common attributes of small economies examined above, it can be postulated that small nations tend to exhibit a higher degree of *globalization* and a higher degree of *flexibility* compared to their larger counterparts in terms of exploiting, reacting, and adjusting to opportunities and challenges in the world economy. Needless to say, these commonalities are closely interrelated and largely complementary with each other[8].

But so long as small open nations are market economies, it is their *individual firms* not their governments (except a nation's exchange rate and inflation management) that make strategic decisions in response to the constraints and opportunities associated with the smallness of their economies. Hence, the connecting link between these two sets of macroeconomic phenomena is microeconomic[9]:

Smallness Characteristics → Firms' strategic Responses → Smallness-specific Globalization.

### 2.2.3 Salient Characteristics of Small Economies

In short, the basic propositions are that small open economies exhibit a *higher degree of globalization* and a *higher degree of flexibility* than their larger counterparts, and ceteris paribus, the degree of globalization and flexibility is basically determined by the extent (measures) of smallness.

Moreover, from the preceding analysis of the characteristics of small economies, it appears that compared to their larger counterparts, small nations, when economically successful and adaptive are:

1. More export focused in manufacturing, particularly in early stages of development,
2. Likely to specialize in differentiated manufactures(niche-market goods in the global market place) as they advance in industrialization,
3. More actively involved with direct overseas businesses, initially by inviting foreign firms to invest in their home markets but soon afterwards by increasingly carrying on their own business operations abroad. That is, changing from a net importer of (a host for) direct business operations to a net exporter of (a home base for) overseas operations[10],
4. More sensitive in strategically managing exchange rates as a macroeconomic instrument of competitiveness for their firms (since what matters for competitiveness is the real exchange rate and not the nominal exchange rate)[11],
5. Likely to be in a better position to achieve price stability (if under a true flexible exchange rate) through the effective use of monetary policy and the strategic management of exchange

rates, which provides a real depreciation without intervening in the foreign exchange market,

6. More actively involved in international trade through varying degrees of economic integration,
7. Likely to have a more homogeneous cultural pattern and a well educated population. Thus, it develops a better environment for the efficient flow of information among government and corporations assisting in the public/private sector complementary relationship.
8. Likely to be in a better position to quickly adapt to uncertainties and external shocks through their higher degree of corporatism, which result in more appropriate macro-economic policies.
9. Likely to exhibit a higher degree of flexibility through other factors such as a simpler language situation and a more even income distribution.

## 2.3 AN UNCONVENTIONAL VIEW OF SMALLNESS[12]

The definition of smallness is admittedly an arbitrary concept, and it is generally agreed that the use of a single variable such as population for this purpose is too narrow a conception. It is true that in economic analysis, nation size is often not taken as the primary leading factor, thus categories such as "newly industrializing," "least developed," "land locked developing," "developed," and "island developing" seem to be more relevant in understanding the economic problems of these countries.

Even Schumacher, a fervent advocate of small sizes, appeared to disregard the relevance of country size, and said: ". . . one might ask, what is the appropriate size of a country? . . . It depends on what we are trying to do." He also said that the viability of a nation is just a problem of people and not size (Schumacher 1973, p.66).

The notion of smallness as used in conventional international economics is defined in terms of the neoclassical model of perfect competition which serves to facilitate a logical analysis of equilibrium forces that cannot help in reflecting on the real world situation:

> "We adopt the usual trade theorist's interpretation of small economy as being one that does not affect the larger economic environment in which it operates. . . . First the small country faces perfectly elastic demand in world markets and trades at exogenously given prices.

> Second, if the small economy trades on world capital markets, it does so at an exogenously given rate of interest Finally, the R&D activities of the small country do not influence the rate of accumulation of knowledge capital in the world at large, either because its investments in knowledge generate no cross-border knowledge spillovers or because the spillovers that it does generate are negligible in magnitude Of course *no real country fits this description of smallness*. Nonetheless, the construct of the small open economy remains a useful one, inasmuch as it allows us to study the channels through which world markets influence domestic behavior without our needing worry initially about the reverse feedback relationships." (emphasis added); (Grossman and Helpman 1991, p. 144)

The above way of defining smallness, though useful in the conventional neoclassical analysis, cannot help us much in reflecting on the actual world situation. Looking at Western Europe, we can immediately see that there are small economies such as Malta, Cyprus, Austria, Finland, Sweden, Denmark, Ireland, Portugal, and Greece, as well as many large ones such as Germany, Italy, France, Great Britain, and Spain, and clearly notice that the size of nations *does matter* in influencing the behaviors of their key constituent economic units—firms—and the pattern of economic activities at the national and international level both in negative and positive terms.

The neoclassical conception of smallness is a static device that facilitates a logical analysis of equilibrating forces; an economic unit is abstracted to be atomistically small, so small—and so insignificant—that it can neither exert any impeding friction to the process of equilibration nor bring about imperfections (infirmities) in the market's ultimate state of allocative equilibrium attainable under the assumption of perfect competition.

The neoclassical definition is thus merely focused on exchanges—resource allocative activities—for which each economic unit becomes a passive price taker in the market, making necessary adjustments only at the margin. It considers neither the *spatial* dimensions of economic activities the word smallness implies in everyday usage; nor does it refer to any dynamic (or strategically maneuvering) changes the smallness of a country compels its firms to make. In fact, a state of perfect competition corresponds to a "firmless" world, in the sense that the firms are assumed to be devoid of any idiosyncratic behavior, since they are made identical under the assumption of perfect knowledge; for example, there is no logical ground regarding where they emerge as multinational corporations. The firms play no strategic or dynamic economic function. This genre of conceptualization is *basically static (mechanistic), marginalism-based, and deductive in reasoning.*

Instead, a different notion of *smallness* is proposed, one based on real world empiricism and reflective of its spatial implications. Simply put, this notion stems from the casual (yet realistic) observation that a small country such as Austria, Belgium, Denmark, or Portugal has *a quite different and distinct set of parametric factors* from that of a large economy such as France, Germany, or Spain; a set of parametric factors that inevitably affects the small economy in some uniquely distinctive ways.

This observation explicitly brings in spatial economic elements in line with Paul Krugman's new emphasis on the geographical factors in economics. As Krugman writes: "By economic geography I mean the location of production in space; that is, that branch of economics that worries about where things happen in relation to one another." (Krugman, 1991, p. 1). Hence, the real-world bounded approach in this study is *more functionally dynamic (behavioral), structuralism-based, and inductive in reasoning.*

According to this interpretation, *smallness means a compactedness of a nation in the domestic economic space:* a nation is confined to a small economic space such that it can and must, if it is raise its economic efficiency and welfare, use its size characteristics strategically in taking advantage of its linkages with the outside world.

Given the practical perspective above, a number of small nations can be identified which satisfy the following criteria:

1. A small domestic market (a small basis for scale economies),
2. A small geographical area (a high geographical compactedness), and
3. A small area-specific paucity of natural resources.

Thus, the fundamental proposition that if small nations exhibit a higher degree of globalization than their larger counterparts, and that ceteris paribus, this degree of globalization is basically determined by a composite measure of smallness, then it can be classified in accordance with these three variables at the macroeconomic level:

MS = Market Size,
GC = Geographical Compactedness, and
RP = Resource Paucity.

Some typical countries of this class in Western Europe are, for example, Austria, Belgium, Denmark, Finland, Greece, Ireland, Luxembourg, the Netherlands, Portugal, and Sweden. These nations are quite different from their larger counterparts such as: France, Great Britain, Germany, Italy, and Spain. But yet, all these economies, large or small, need to take advantage of their division of labor and dynamic comparative advantage in order to become economically successful.

## 2.4 SUMMARY

Many definitions have been used to determine the size of nations, but economists dealing with the subject of smallness do not have a conventional definition of what it means. This chapter has provided a literature review on the notion of smallness and has revealed the lack of consensus when determining the size of nations. It has also provided the salient characteristics of small open economies, and an unconventional view of smallness with an approach more functionally dynamic and inductive in reasoning.

Finally, the conceptual analysis leads to the conclusion that compared to their larger counterparts, small nations are more globalized. The first part of the following chapter of this book will be devoted to the specific approaches to globalization to overcome smallness and to secure economic growth.

CHAPTER 3

# Globalization and Structural Adaptability

## To Overcome Smallness and Secure Economic Growth

Growth theory has treated countries as if they were self-sufficient islands. Extensions of the theory to a world of international trade and capital flows have been left as obscure exercises for neoclassical math wizards. This practice is no longer acceptable, especially when dealing with the economic growth of small open economies.

Section 3.1 looks at the small countries' specific approaches to globalization to overcome smallness and to secure economic growth and will be divided into six sub-sections. These are: trade focus, specialization in "niche-market" goods, involvement in direct overseas businesses, sensitivity in managing exchange rates, price stability, and economic integration in the world economy.

Additionally, export growth is often considered to be a main determinant of production and employment growth of small open economies. This so called export-led growth can be sustained by the foreign exchange made available by export growth. This also facilitates the importation of capital goods which increases the production potential of a small nation, and secondly the volume of and the competition on export markets results in economies of scale and an acceleration of technical progress in production, as emphasized by the New or Endogenous Growth Theory[13].

Two ways of globalization that small open economies have employed successfully to overcome smallness are the creation of dynamic comparative advantages and the integration into world markets, both of which for dynamic increasing returns to scale. For example, Denmark has been successful at acquiring leading positions in some high-technology industries. Furthermore, it holds the number one position in the competitiveness ranking of European countries. And Portugal is beginning to specialize in human-capital intensive industries, already being in front of Spain and Italy in terms of the competitiveness European ranking (World Competitiveness Report 1993, p. 15).

While it may be obvious that knowledge always flows rapidly around the globe, the reality is quite different. For example, the concentration of high-technology industries in the U.S. in Silicon Valley and Route 128 suggests that some benefits exist from physical proximity to other researchers. The same happens in small open economies where new ideas tend to be spread more efficiently by skilled personnel due to their geographical compactedness and smallness (Krugman 1991, Chapter 2).

Grossman and Helpman (1991, Chapter 8) argue that the existence of technological externalities plays an important role in the determination of dynamic comparative advantage. Such spillovers may be the necessary ingredients that can generate a self-perpetuating process for technological dominance. Again, small open economies may benefit more from these technological externalities than their larger counterparts, since the small economies have stronger trade/FDI orientations. Thus the creation of dynamic comparative advantages is facilitated.

As discussed above, growth theory is changing directions somewhat. In both growth theories, technology seems to be the main determinant of growth. Indeed, not just organizational change at the firm level, but also institutional change at the macro level needs to be included in this framework. Then, growth can be interpreted as dependent on both technical and institutional change.

Hence, Section 3.2 looks at the institutional flexibility of small nations to overcome smallness and to secure economic growth. Again, this section will be divided in three sub-sections: economic flexibility, public and private complementary relationship, and corporatism. This study tells us that small open economies tend to have higher degrees of: flexibility, complementary public/private ties, and corporatism, than their larger counterparts.

Based on the analysis of Sections 3.1 and 3.2, some basic propositions will be extracted and later tested in Chapter Four. And finally, a summary will conclude the chapter.

## 3.1 SPECIFIC APPROACHES OF GLOBALIZATION TO OVERCOME SMALLNESS AND TO SECURE ECONOMIC GROWTH[14]

This section derives the prominent characteristics of small open economies based on the previous conceptual analysis. Hence, it is well established that compared to their larger counterparts, small economies when economically successful tend to be: (1) more export focused in manufacturing, particularly in early stages of development; (2) likely to specialize in differentiated manufactures (niche-market goods in the global market place) as they advance in industrialization; (3) more actively involved with direct overseas businesses; (4) more sensitive in strategically managing exchange rates as a macroeconomic instrument of competitiveness for its firms; (5) likely to be in a better position to achieve price stability and; (6) more actively involved in international trade through varying degrees of economic integration.

In other words, small countries are more "globalized" in terms of the above measures of exploiting the opportunities in the global economy. Needless to say, these characteristics are closely interrelated and largely complementary with each other. In what follows, the smallness-induced behaviors and characteristics of globalization will be explored.

### 3.1.1 Trade (Export-Import) Focus

Trade has long been known as an engine of growth. In fact, exports are usually considered more primary than imports, since the former serve as a means of earning foreign exchange with which to purchase imports. Exports are less likely to be impeded, although imports are usually subject to all sorts of restrictions. Indeed, "asymmetrical trade" (free exports but somewhat restricted imports) may be a more powerful engine of growth than complete free trade.

For example, the economic miracles of the Asian NIEs (newly industrializing economies), which fit our definition of small economies, have been in significant part credited to their high export orientation. Small European nations such as Denmark, Belgium, the Netherlands, and Austria, similarly exhibit high trade to GDP ratios.

In the Ricardian doctrine of comparative advantage, the size of nations does not matter. But the size of nations plays a critical role in the Smithian doctrine of absolute advantage in which scale economies, the dynamic learning effect, and the spillovers of knowledge determine the costs of production, hence price competitiveness. Thus, a small domestic market means a disadvantage. Indeed, Adam Smith (1776) over two hundred years ago, already regarded trade as an extension of the domestic market, thus providing a basis for scale-based production and learning benefits. Smith was clearly conscious of the spatial dimensions of economic activities, but Ricardo turned trade theory into a spaceless/distanceless construct.

Two stylized cases may be distinguished; one is the situation in which export markets serve as *marginal* (small) supplements in scale economies, the other as *structural* (substantially large) supplements. Even a large domestic market may still benefit from trade if additional output further reduces production costs. This is best illustrated by America's automobile industry; the huge domestic market alone used to be sufficiently large to provide a basis for scale economies, but because of the invasion of the domestic market by imports, Detroit now has to depend on exports to maintain an adequate basis for scale economies. Yet exports are basically still only marginal supplements.

On the other hand, an extremely small domestic market compels the firms to look for markets outside the country. Without exports, they are unable to survive, because the production costs would not go down to a competitive level. Export sales thus serve as structural supplements. As will be discussed later, this distinction in the role of exports between marginal and structural supplements has an important effect on a nation's exchange rate management.

Besides, the smallness of nations is usually associated with a paucity of natural resources at home. In addition to export dependence, small economies are also likely to become more dependent on imports than large economies. For example, Austria, Belgium, Greece, and Portugal are highly dependent on imports in the aggregate, since they lack some specific natural resources (e.g., grain).

Many economists have analyzed the relationship between exports and economic growth for different countries (small and large) in diverse stages of industrialization, among them; Balassa (1978), Chow (1987), Sephton (1989), Kohli and Singh (1989), Sarkar and Singer (1991), Dodaro (1991), Esfahani (1991), Grossman and Helpman (1991), and Kugler (1991). But there is no consensus among them about the view of export-led growth[15]. The issue of exports and growth will be explored further and the question of whether small nations tend to be more trade oriented than their counterparts and therefore, have a relatively higher degree of correlation between exports and GNP, will be tested.

For example, Balassa's study (1978, p. 185) of a group of eleven developing countries that had already established an industrial base showed that an increase in the rate of growth of exports of one percent tended to raise the rate of growth of GNP between .06 and .07 of 1 percent. Furthermore, Esfahani (1991, p. 93 & 110) writes: "Export promotion policies as a superior development strategy for semi-industrialized countries have found support in the statistically significant correlations established between export expansion and output growth." (p. 93). The estimation results reported indicate that in a country with an export to GDP ratio of .21, (which is the median for the sample), a one percent increase in the rate of growth of exports during the 1973–1981 period could have raised the GDP growth rate by .057 percent. The results are similar to Balassa's results between of .06 and .07 percent. Based on these results, for the European Union members with a mean export GNP ratio of .38 during the same period 1973–1981, a one percent increase in the rate of growth of exports should have raised the GNP growth rate by more than .057 percent (assuming that whether a nation is semi-industrialized or a industrialized does not affect the outcome).

Recently, Kugler (1991, p. 82) in his study of six industrialized nations using the statistical technique of cointegration[16] testing for a long run relationship between GDP and exports concludes that the hypothesis that exports can be excluded from the cointegrating relations must not be rejected for three of the countries, which provides mixed results concerning the importance of exports for GDP. Thus, there is only weak empirical evidence supporting the view of export-led growth. The fact that the countries used in the study were large nations should be pointed out.

It also should be noted that the so called "East Asian Miracle" is attributed in part to the export push (manufactured exports) and rapid growth of exports by which these countries have attained high rates of productivity through new technologies and innovation; emphasized by the New Growth Theory. In addition, some small Western European economies such as Malta, Cyprus, Greece, and Portugal have enjoyed high rates of economic growth in part to the export push as well. Manufactured export growth provides a powerful mechanism for technological upgrading in imperfect world technology markets. Since companies that export have greater access to better technology, there are both benefits to the firm and spillovers to the rest of the economy that are not reflected in market transactions. These positive externalities (information related) are an important source of rapid productivity growth, especially for small newly industrializing economies catching up to the new technologies developed by the advanced and large economies (World Bank, 1993, p. 23).

*Proposition 1:* Nation size does matter when it comes to trade. Small economies naturally grow more trade-oriented in both exports and imports, particularly when exports are based on Smithian absolute advantages obtainable from scale economies and learning effect and when imports are based on absolute availability. Ceteris paribus, small nations thus become more trade-focused than large ones (e.g., a high ratio of trade—exports plus imports—to GNP).

### 3.1.2 Specialization in "Niche-Market" Goods

The firms in small open economies, being confronted with a limit of the domestic market, must pursue diversification in both products and markets. Product diversification leads them to focus on niche-market goods in the world market, whereas market diversification means the development of overseas markets as structural supplements for domestic markets—hence, both avenues of diversification are highly complementary and augmented[17]. Indeed, this complementary relationship jibes with the imperfect competition theory of trade (Krugman 1990); so long as the differentiated products manufactured by small country firms appeal to the consumers in the world economy, exporting provides a basis for scale economies, making their competitiveness self-fulfilling[18].

Furthermore, Becker (1994) supports the proposition when he writes that economic efficiency in small economies forces them to concentrate on a few products, thus they specialize in niches that are too small for a larger economy. "Small nations are proliferating because economies can prosper by producing niche goods and services for world markets" (Becker 1994, p. 20).

*Proposition 2:* Small country manufactures are more likely to concentrate on the niche markets of the world economy by way of product differentiation as they succeed in industrialization. At the macroeconomic level, this may mean a higher degree of intra-industry trade.

### 3.1.3 Involvement in Direct Overseas Businesses

Direct overseas businesses involve foreign direct investment (FDI), licensing agreements, managerial and marketing contracts, joint research activities, and other non equity type of cross-border activities in both directions, inward as well as outward. In this section and throughout the book, the focus will be on FDI alone[19]. This raises two questions. First, does nation size have some influence on the nature and extent of FDI? And second, does FDI enhance economic growth in small economies?

Small open economies that stress trade as an engine of growth are likely to get involved in direct business operations abroad much earlier in their developmental history and to a much greater extent than their large counterparts. Exporters from small nations need to build marketing infrastructure abroad in the much earlier phases of sales expansion and to a much greater proportion than at home because of their heavier dependency on exports (a case of structural supplements).

Furthermore, as mentioned above, they are likely to focus on the niche markets in the global economy as a corporate strategy during the course of exploiting overseas markets. The more niche-market oriented, the greater the need to provide customer-specific services in the overseas markets; hence the more strongly induced to engage in direct overseas business activities.

Small nation manufacturers, particularly in vertically integrated industries, may become more dependent on outsourcing of intermediate goods abroad than large ones, but because of market imperfections in the forms of "the horrors of bilateral monopoly" and "fluctuating exchange rates," they are motivated to resort to FDI (internalization) instead of trade (Niehans, 1977).

Although FDI through multinational corporations plays a crucial role as a transplanter of technology, skills, and access to the world markets, these multinationals also facilitate structural upgrading and economic growth in small developing countries (Ozawa 1992, p.27). According to Ozawa's (1992) dynamic paradigm of FDI and economic growth, there are three basic principles involved in the process: trade augmentation through FDI, increasing factor incongruity, and localized learning and technological accumulation. Any small developing economy must open its economy to trade and interact with and learn from the already advanced economies in order to raise its standard of living.

For example, an important factor in East Asia's successful productivity-based catching up, as well as for Greece and Portugal, was and still is the openness to foreign ideas and technology by encouraging foreign companies to invest in the region. The benefits of FDI can be substantial in a small economy, particularly in generating foreign exchange and employment. Foreign investment projects themselves can contribute to building know-how in a small open economy where there is a shortage of skilled labor and managerial ability. Also as investments mature and local and regional linkages are fortified, multinationals that are often thought of as "footloose" will stay, and the positive spillovers created by successful ventures will encourage more investment.

On a macro level, small economies' high propensity to engage in direct overseas businesses implies a shift in the "development-path" function of net outward investment introduced by Dunning (1981). This function (U-curve) which measures a net outward investment position (on the Y-axis) as a function of per capita income (on the X-axis) is likely to shift *inward* for small open economies relative to large economies, because the former proportionally are more dependent on inward investment in their early stages of development and then become more strongly oriented to outward investment as they advance in economic development.

*Proposition 3:* Small open economies tend to develop direct business links (such as FDI, licensing, subcontracting, and other forms of investment) in the earlier stages of development and to a much greater extent both as a home and host country than their large counterparts.

### 3.1.4 Strategic Management and Use of Exchange Rates

Exchange rates are the connecting links between domestic prices and the global prices. The more "globally oriented" a country is, the more sensitively and strategically it manages and uses the exchange rate mechanism. In other words, the exchange rate is one of the principal policy variables for small open economies. Obviously, what really matters for international competitiveness is not the nominal exchange rate but rather the real exchange rate. The real exchange rate—whether home currency is undervalued or overvalued—directly affects the profitability of domestic (home) producers of tradeable goods and services, since it creates both the subsidy and tax effects on such tradeables.

### *3.1.4.1 Real Depreciation*

Hence, the hypotheses is that small (trade oriented) economies, as compared to their large counterparts, are more likely to manage macroeconomic variables in such a way as to prevent their home currencies from becoming overvalued. There are some interesting pieces of evidence that this is the case with Europe's small economies. De Grauwe and Vanhaverbeke (1990) found that there existed large divergences in the exchange rate experiences of small versus large EMS (European Monetary System) nations over the 1979–1988 period. In their study, the small economies are Belgium, the Netherlands, and Denmark. All three small nations experienced a real depreciation of their currencies (vis-a-vis the U.S. dollar), which was much larger than a change in the nominal exchange rate, notably over the 1979–1983 period. For example, the nominal exchange rate for Belgium depreciated by 17.0 percent, but its real exchange rate depreciated by 28.0 percent; despite the nominal rate appreciation of 2.5 percent for the Netherlands, its real rate depreciated as much as 18.0 percent; and for Denmark, the nominal rate depreciated by 17.2 percent, but the real rate depreciated even further by as much as 21.8 percent. In contrast, large EMS nations' changes in real exchange rates remained much smaller; "In the large EMS countries we generally do not observe the same large real depreciations as in the small countries. The real effective exchange rates of the large EMS countries exhibit changes, which remain within a band of approximately plus and minus 10 percent" (De Grauwe and Vanhaverbeke, 1990, p. 139).

The most significant disturbances at that time were the second oil shock of 1979–80 and the subsequent world recession of 1981–82, which both affected small open economies more adversely than large EMS economies. The small nations needed larger real depreciations in order to weather the storms of the tandem external disturbances; therefore, they must have adopted appropriate policy measures to keep the exchange rates undervalued[20].

### *3.1.4.2 Pricing to Market: A Strategic Behavior*

In addition, small nations that are heavily dependent on trade (e.g., exports serve as structural supplements) are more likely to adopt the practice of "pricing to market" than large nations (for whom exports are mostly marginal supplements). By "pricing to market" is meant a strategic pricing of exports which may be contrary to the conventional wisdom related to changes in the exchange rate. The conventional wisdom says that when their home currency depreciates, exporting firms decrease their export prices in the overseas markets, and when their home currency appreciates, they increase export prices. In other words, the conventional wisdom postulates a "pass-through" effect. But, when pricing to market (PTM) occurs, the pass-through mechanism is thrown out of kilter.

Krugman (1987) ties this nonconventional phenomenon, PTM, to the features of market structure (imperfect competition) and dynamic adjustment effects. His explanations about pricing behaviors are given in terms of whether a change in the exchange rate is *temporary* or *permanent*, how the demand will respond, how fast the supply can adjust to meet an increase in demand, and whether companies' reputation about advertised prices is at stake. In addition, he fits the "monopolistic competition" theory of trade nicely with the PTM phenomenon; the more differentiated and niche-market-focused a product is, the less price sensitive it remains, thereby earning excess profits generated with a depreciation of home currency.

If a form of PTM behavior occurs, different prices (two sets of prices) will necessarily appear for tradeable goods at home and abroad. Throop (1994) presented evidence—and concluded—that such price discrimination is less worth while for American producers who operate in a large domestic market and whose foreign markets represent a relatively small proportion of total sales (i.e., a case of exports as marginal supplements). It may then be argued that this type of strategic price discrimination is worth taking for exporters from a small open economy who derive a large proportion of total sales from foreign markets. In other words, they practice PTM more actively than their counterparts in large economies.

*Proposition 4:* Small open economies are more sensitive in managing their exchange rate regimes as an instrument of competitiveness, and those small-country firms which produce niche-market goods usually resort to PTM to reap exchange gains (i.e., they internalize the benefits of exchange gains created by their country's exchange rate management).

### 3.1.5 Inflation, Price Stability, and Exchange Rates

Inflation is an old and long debated economic phenomena which has afflicted nations throughout history. For example, the discovery of the New World in the XV century and the exploitation of American gold by Spanish authorities brought to Spain, and the rest of Europe, a new wave of inflation lasting until the mid XVII century. In recent times, inflation has been identified primarily with war periods such as World War I and II, the Korean War, and the Vietnam War. And in the last twenty years, inflation has been linked to political instability in places like in the Middle East, Latin America, and Eastern Europe[21].

First, a theoretical explanation of the inflationary process will be provided.

#### *3.1.5.1 International Monetarist Theories on Inflation*

The explanation of overall price levels has always presented a problem for economists. One of the difficulties arises from the fundamental proposition that, in equilibrium, economic outcomes do not depend on the absolute level of prices. Thus inflation, if an economy is fully adapted to it, has few if any real effects. Furthermore, it seems that price instability feeds on itself, and that *expectations* of inflation can sometimes give the best explanation for it.

The "Quantity Theory of Money" advocates that the price level is determined by an exogenously given supply of money[22]. Then it looks like managing inflation is just an elementary process of controlling the money supply. The *Quantity Theory* does not provide a theory of inflation but only of nominal income. The so called "Natural Rate Hypothesis" gives a more complete depiction by offering a theory of real output (Boltho 1982). This postulate seems to be in accordance with the neo-classical view of the operation of the labor market in which demand and supply for labor depend on real wages and not nominal wages[23].

Another theory which explains the domestic price level is found on exchange rate alignments under "Purchasing Power Parity." Also an important distinction needs to be made between a system of fixed or flexible exchange rates. In the case of flexible exchange rates, a change in money supply that leads to absolute but not relative price changes at home implies that the relative price of domestic goods and of foreign tradeable goods also remained unchanged[24]. Then, the price adjustment comes from a variation of the exchange rate. Thus, the exchange rate changes to maintain constant relative prices with foreign goods.

In the case of fixed exchange rates problems arise. If the money supply increases, so do domestic prices. But if foreign prices remain the same and if the exchange rate is fixed, a change in domestic prices will change relative prices as well. The solution to the problem then is that domestic money supply cannot change; therefore, under fixed exchange rates an economy cannot control its money supply. There is a contrast between flexible and fixed exchange rates. Under the first system, a nation can choose its money supply growth and its rate of inflation; under the latter a country loses control over its money growth and its inflation rate.

#### *3.1.5.2 Inflationary Forces and Pressures*

It may be more appropriate to try to identify the forces that lead to inflationary pressures. These are said to be of two types: demand-pull and cost-push forces. Demand-pull inflation may be determined by the extent of unemployment[25] and the degree of capacity utilization. Cost-push inflation may be detected through wage pressures and import prices. These pressures do not lie so much in the initial stage but in the inflexibility of the economic system which eventually turns the push into a spiral of rising prices and wages. Small countries tend to be more flexible than their larger counterparts; therefore, they are able to mitigate the push before it becomes a spiral of rising prices.

Another force of inflationary pressures and price instability is the struggle over income distribution, as characterized by conflicts between distribution of capital and labor, the private and the public sector, and different lobbying groups in society. Again, small economies tend to have less unequal income distribution than their larger counterparts, thus decreasing such social tensions, which does moderate inflationary pressures.

Even though control of money supply and strategic management of exchange rates help small nations to price their products competitively and alleviate inflationary pressures, it is important to point out that inflationary problems appear also deeply rooted in the social, political, and institutional structures of economies, especially in Europe, and its control is ultimately a domestic problem. It appears that the extent of the difficulty differs among nations, and the appropriate policy response may differ as well.

### *3.1.5.3 The European Case since the Collapse of Bretton Woods*

European monetary history since the Second World War has been a continuous process of Europe affirming its own identity despite recurring crises. The main element of conflict in the 1990's is and probably will be throughout this decade, the adjustment to the increasing weight of the German economy, in particular the power of the Bundesbank in determining monetary policy within European boundaries. It seems the same conflict existed under the Bretton Woods System where there was an asymmetric system of fixed, but adjustable, exchange rates. The United States fixed the price of gold and guaranteed the convertability of dollar assets held by other central banks into gold at the specified rate. In exchange the other countries agreed to hold dollars as reserve assets and guaranteed the stability of the exchange rate.

The period of exchange rate instability after the demise of the Bretton Woods System was a grim age for monetary cooperation in Europe. Furthermore, when in autumn 1973 the first oil shock quadrupled oil prices, the monetary cohesion of Europe became even weaker. Collignon, Bofinger, Johnson, and de Maigret (1994, p. 12) write: "Within the snake two groups of weak and strong currency countries had emerged, reflecting different target preferences for monetary and economic policies. Germany and the smaller countries in the DM zone (Netherlands, Norway) gave preference to domestic monetary stability, while France, Italy, Belgium/Luxembourg, Denmark, and Sweden aimed for bridging strategies which made them prone to higher inflation. . . . Soon a vicious circle between spiralling prices (12–15 percent inside the snake, 20 percent outside) and devaluing exchange rates developed[26]."

The European Monetary System was created in 1978 as a remedy for exchange rate instability and as a push toward closer monetary cooperation. Again, the EMS, as Bretton Woods, was and still is a fixed, but adjustable, exchange rate system[27].

Based on the simple monetarist approach stated above, one would expect to find inflation rates in the European Union clustering fairly closely together. In other words, there should not be a statistical difference between small and large economies' inflation rates. Furthermore, Caravelis (1994, p. 41) writes that as to price stability in the European Union in 1993, the three best performing nations—three small nations—were Denmark, with the lowest inflation rate of 1.4

percent, followed by The Netherlands with an inflation rate of 2.1 percent, and Ireland with 2.3 percent, the third best performing. On the contrary, the two worst performing nations—two small nations as well—were Portugal with an inflation rate of 6.7 percent, and Greece with 13.7 percent being more than three and a half times higher than the European Union inflation rate average of 3.8 percent[28]. This performance perhaps could be explained by domestic structural problems in Portugal and Greece.

At the same time, it is important to ask the question as to whether there are significant differences between small and large European nations in their ability to control inflation by effectively adapting to changes in world economic conditions via flexible institutions, implementing sound macroeconomic policies, and successfully managing and coping with socio-economic and political problems (i.e., wage bargaining influenced by the degree of corporatism). It seems that small open economies do show a higher degree of flexibility, a higher successful rate in implementing macroeconomic policies, and a higher degree of corporatism. Consequently, it could be asserted that small open economies, outside the European Union, with the characteristics stated above, and the ability to effectively use monetary policy and to manage exchange rates under a flexible exchange rate system, are in a better position to manage and control inflation than their larger counterparts. For example according to Wood (1992, p. 26 & 39), Singapore, a small open economy with the highest international trade/GDP ratio in the world, has enjoyed great success since the collapse of the Breton Woods System in controlling inflation through close control of its money stock and letting its exchange rate rise relative to larger countries with higher levels of inflation. He concludes that Singapore's success in achieving price stability is not due entirely to monetary discipline but is also enhanced by a total macroeconomic approach that avoids excesses in wage policies, socio-economic conflicts, and budget deficits, while protecting and stimulating domestic industries.

*Proposition 5:* Small open economies, under a truly flexible exchange rate, are in a better position to attain price stability through the effective use of monetary policy and the strategic management of exchange rates than their larger counterparts.

### 3.1.6 International Economic Integration

An obvious question is whether the drawbacks of smallness can be overcome by economic integration[29]. The experience here is disappointing. The European Union is perhaps the most successful attempt at economic integration in recent times, perhaps the ASEAN concord may indeed develop into an important and permanent regional organization in the near future. NAFTA may become an important free trade area but the three member countries, U.S.A., Canada, and Mexico are considered large rather than small economies. But most of the evidence for developing countries, and for some advanced ones, points to disintegration. The European Free Trade Association, EFTA, the East African Community, EAC, the West African Economic Community, the Caribbean Community, the Andean Pact, the Latin American Free Trade Association, LAFTA, and the Central American Common Market are evidence of the difficulties of regional cooperation. The more advanced and large members do not want to be taxed for the benefit of the less advanced, and the poorer and smaller members feel that they will lose out from the location of industry, migration of skilled workers and professionals, and capital movements, all of which will gravitate toward the more advanced, sometimes also the bigger, regions. Among more advanced countries powerful centrifugal forces are at work in Yugoslavia, and some of the Commonwealth Independent States (CIS), along with weaker forces in Canada, United Kingdom, and Spain.

Groups of people with a national conscience but without a state of their own fight to become independent states. If these groups are successful in their aspirations to become independent from their central governments[30], more nation states will be looking for trading partners and new economic regions will become integrated[31].

Furthermore as the European Union strengthens and fortifies its position in the world economy, other small European nations will want to become a part of it, thus increasing the integrated economic space of Europe. This tendency has already begun since three small European nations, Austria, Finland, and Sweden, became members of the European Union in 1995. Also, some other European nations have shown an interest such as: Hungary, Poland, Slovakia, the Czech Republic, Turkey, Bulgaria, Romania, Albania, Slovenia, Malta, and Cyprus. Even Switzerland may be forced to become a part of it, so it will not be discriminated against by the rest of Europe. Moreover, the

Baltic states of Latvia, Estonia, and Lithuania have already shown interest in joining the European Union as well.

### *3.1.6.1 The Global Experience and the Motives of Small Nations for Economic Integration*

Since the end of the Second World War various forms of economic integration have been implemented. Many of them were formed by small economies. The EC, the most significant and influential example of economic integration in the world, was founded by six nations under the Treaty of Rome in 1957. Out of the original six, three fit the definition of small economies for this study. These are Belgium, Luxembourg, and the Netherlands. After new additions to the EU throughout the years, the Union is now comprised of fifteen nations, of which ten can be considered small economies. These are Austria, Greece, the Netherlands, Portugal, Denmark, Finland, Belgium, Ireland, Sweden, and Luxembourg. Thus two thirds of the countries forming the European Union are small nations.

EFTA is the other major scheme of economic integration in Western Europe, but it is in a severe decline. This program originated thanks to the UK in the 1950's, when it was not ready to commit itself to the European Community[32]. The outcome was EFTA which was established in 1960 by the Stockholm Convention with the object of creating a free market for industrial products only. The members were Austria, Denmark, Norway, Sweden, Switzerland, and the UK. Finland and Iceland joined later. Again, six out of eight members were small economies (El-Agraa 1982, p. 3–5).

But Denmark and the UK joined the EC in 1973, and Austria, Finland, and Sweden joined the EU in 1995. This has left EFTA with a membership consisting of very few nations. Simply by examining the different economic integrations in Western Europe, it can be concluded that smaller economies recognize the need to join a large trading scheme to overcome smallness.

Also, looking at other economic integration schemes, it can be observed the same as in the European experience. In the West African Economic Community, all the original nations can be considered small (again based on the four main control variables). These are Ivory Coast, Upper Volta, Mali, Mauritania, Niger, and Senegal. In the Caribbean Community, most of the members can be considered mini-states with the exception of Barbados, Guyana, Jamaica, and Trinidad and Tobago, which again fit the definition of small economies. In another international economic integration, the Central American Common Market, all members again—Costa Rica, El Salvador, Guatemala, Honduras, and Nicaragua—are small economies (El-Agraa, 1982).

Now the question is: Why do most economic integration schemes have a majority membership of smaller economies rather than large ones?[33] As mentioned previously, small open economies, due to their smaller domestic market, have certain disadvantages. These include: (1) the smaller area is not conducive to a concentration of products with a comparative advantage (Switzerland is a major exception) (2) a small domestic market gives no chance to reap the benefits of scale and scope economies, (3) smallness brings no bargaining power in the economic international arena, (4) small countries tend to develop monopolies due to lack of competition within the region, and finally (5) there is a lack of resources to be devoted to R&D.

Thus, a small open economy which becomes part of an international economic integration concord enjoys the possibility of eliminating its size disadvantages by reaping the following economic gains:

1. Enhanced efficiency in the production process by increased specialization, thus gaining dynamic comparative advantage in more products.
2. Increased production targets by enjoying scale economies due to the increased size of the market. For example, Austria, Finland, and Sweden have increased their markets from less than 10 million to more than 350 million after joining the EU in 1995.
3. A tremendous improvement in international bargaining position made possible by the larger size. For example, Denmark would have rarely been able to influence any international economic decision. But as Thurow (1992) points out, there is a new economic game being played in this new economic world with the U.S., Japan, and the EC as the primary players, and Denmark forms part of one of the participants.
4. Enforced positive changes in economic efficiency and availability of goods and services due to an increase in area-wide competition, and finally
5. Changes affecting both the amount and quality of the factors of production due to technological advances and innovation.

> Krugman (1990, p. 166–167) explores this issue by introducing the Schumpeterian paradigm of growth with an economy characterized by dynamic increasing returns in which international integration increases the incentives for and the benefits from innovation.

*Proposition 6:* Small open economies tend to be more actively involved in international trade through varying degrees of economic integration to possibly eliminate their size disadvantages by reaping the economic gains of increased specialization, scale economies, technological advances and innovation, increased competition, and increased international bargaining power than their larger counterparts.

## 3.2 STRUCTURAL ADAPTABILITY TO OVERCOME SMALLNESS AND TO SECURE ECONOMIC GROWTH

As small economies become more dependent on international trade for their economic well-being, they tend to become more globalized to exploit the opportunities that the world economy may provide by expanding new trade partners and new markets for their products and pricing them competitively.

International competitiveness of small nations may be secured by strategically managing the exchange rate and assuring price stability. Additionally, international competitiveness to some degree is a matter of institutional flexibility and macro-corporatism. It is known that competitiveness requires change, compromise, and flexibility, which depends in part on the complementary relationship between government and corporations.

### 3.2.1 A Flexible Small Open Economy

It turns out that in a small open economy institutions matter even more than in larger economies. The economic environment that surrounds a small nation may change much more rapidly than for a large one due to the fact that small economies tend to be much more trade dependent.

For example, even tastes can be imported. The so-called "American way of life" has had a tremendous effect on consumer preferences all over the globe, especially in Western European countries. This importance of the milieu factor naturally means that the small open economy has to adapt quickly to foreign developments. It *must* be flexible. Hence, flexibility is more of a necessity for a small country than for a large one.

Killick (1993, p. 47) defines a flexible economy: "As one in which ends and means are quickly adjusted to changing constraints and opportunities. This includes flexibility in the institutional base of the socio-economic system, as well as flexibility on the part of government policy."

Small open economies, if they are to be successful in quickly adjusting to changing economic conditions, need to have an efficient informational and incentive system. Imperfect information—consequently a high level of transactions costs—is a main culprit for the lack of economic flexibility, especially in larger economies. Information must be fed into decision systems and translated into rewards and penalties that will induce appropriate responses. Small developed nations stand a better chance to achieve efficient information flows due to fewer institutional layers in the system.

*Proposition 7:* Nation size does matter when it comes to competitiveness in trade. Small open economies require technological and institutional innovativeness to attain flexibility, particularly to endure external shocks. Ceteris paribus, small nations should exhibit a higher degree of flexibility than their larger counterparts.

### 3.2.2 Public and Private Enterprises: In Search of a Complementary Relationship.

We are all familiar with the state's economic role in terms of its responsibility to correct for or to eliminate market failures such as failures of competition, externalities, incomplete markets, imperfect information, public goods, poverty and inequality, and macroeconomic instability. This section will go a step further in dealing with institutional flexibility and economic globalization, which is requiring national governments, especially those of small nations, to reappraise their domestic macro-organizational strategies[34].

During the 1980's, the role of the government was seriously questioned. The conservative vision of economics, according to which public interventions are nothing but barriers to a free market economy, largely dominated the decade. However, the instability of today's economic world suggests that less government did not bring the anticipated results of the free markets and Adam Smith's *invisible hand.*

Government intervention is once again being reconsidered by many economists. There is a need for guiding economic policies to strengthen domestic competitiveness and to bring stability to the markets. Moreover, there is a need to achieve coordination inside companies, among companies, and most importantly, between companies and the government.

It is evident that with the exception of Hong Kong, the Asian-style development strategies favor active involvement of governments in orchestrating economic policies, and in this they are similar to the 'Nordic economic model.' Both, however, are in conflict with the Western advice of "laissez faire."

Ozawa (1994) suggests further exploration of the role of government and its macro-organizational strategy to achieve technological and institutional innovativeness. Moreover, Ozawa (1987, p. 53) argues the following point concerning the industrial composition of a mature economy: "As innovation is crucial for future growth (New Growth Theory's argument) and positive adjustment, there is no doubt that governments have an important role to play in promoting creative investment and new technological developments."

Also, the small nations' higher degree of economic interdependence compared to their larger counterparts increases the pressure and urgency for these countries to first analyze and second to successfully implement macro-economic and macro-organizational strategies within specific sectors of their economies. These strategies are focused particularly on providing and retaining market niches for highly specialized manufactures in export markets, on which they depend heavily for their economic growth[35].

According to the New Growth Theory, the main ingredient of economic growth is technological innovation, which in fact induces institutional flexibility and/or structural innovation and vice versa. At the same time, this dynamic comparative advantage created by technological progress—crucial to the competitiveness of a small economy—can be hindered by the market imperfections surrounding these man-made created assets. Dunning (1992) writes:

> "The competitiveness of countries is becoming increasingly dependent upon their ability to create new assets; but in order to do so, firms domiciled in one country may need to extend their markets and their supply capabilities into other countries that offer the greatest commercial opportunities." (p. 15).

> "Globalization is leading to increasing competition between firms and industries—and hence between countries—in which these firms and industries are located, producing similar products." (p. 21).
>
> "Large governments often fail to optimize the economies of common governance of their own macro-organizational strategies." (p. 25).

Hence, it is crucial, for small open economies, to use healthy macro-economic management, but also to employ macro-organizational approaches such as: providing an efficient economic environment, developing public infrastructure, increasing innovation by supporting the science and technology sectors, and promoting company exports in order to strengthen this so-called *complementary* relationship between both public and private sectors[36].

These new ties will most likely be successful in those nations where institutional flexibility[37] will be able to attract new capital, labor, and entrepreneurship (inward FDI) to create dynamic comparative advantages through the development of new products and technologies in order to concentrate on the niche-markets of their world

#### *3.2.2.1 Government Implementation of Strategic Policies*

Macro-organizational policies are a response that has been adopted particularly by a number of small open European economies. Thus, it can be said that smallness and openness have brought to the forefront the need for governments to play a more decisive role within their economies. The growing internationalization of the world economy has left these economies even more vulnerable to fluctuations in international economic activity, exchange rates, and commodity prices.

The governments of these nations need to place greater emphasis on strategies to strengthen public and private ties and to support and promote the exporting sector[38] by providing an efficient economic environment, supplying good infrastructure, increasing support and incentives for the science and technology sectors of the economy, and sustaining and promoting the export sector.

1. *An efficient economic environment.* There are three major issues that the government needs to address in this area. First, it is the government's role to set an honest and corruption-free environment for business to follow. Rules and regulations must be clear and have to be enforced. Such practices provide more predictability and less

uncertainty to corporations in terms of cost and time taken to get things done. Second, the government needs to encourage more competition within the domestic economy, in particular among private corporations and also against government owned companies. And finally, the state must be committed to investing in its people to help them achieve their full potential to become productive members of society.

2. *Good infrastructure.* Eric Bridgen, Group Chief Executive at Acer Group Limited writes: "Infrastructure is a key input into a country's overall competitiveness. It provides the basic facilities and raw materials with which companies can undertake their business and, in particular, gain access to markets, customers, and suppliers." (World Competitiveness Report 1993, p. 279). Small nations must give higher priority to those projects which improve productivity or reduce costs. Good infrastructure provides an advantage for business activity and international trade, but alone will not ensure economic success.

3. *Support and incentives for the science and technology sectors.* Technological progress is considered endogenous by the New Growth Theory, and is a direct result of proactive policy actions by both the government and the private sector within the economy. The creation of knowledge is imperative for small economies, but making use of it is equally important. Thus, cooperation between industry and public and private universities through contract research may actually link the gap between theory and practice and facilitate the use of knowledge.

Furthermore, innovation by industry requires an effective complementary role of the government in providing support through adequate infrastructure such as high quality educational system, hardware infrastructure, network of suppliers, financial backing, and a growing demand. It seems obvious that innovation and technological progress require a strategic plan incorporating science, educational, and industrial policy[39].

Such an action plan could include encouraging industrial research, spreading knowledge about new technologies, enhancing major research programs in semi-conductors and electronics, bringing companies closer together to foster the development of environmental industries, and training programs to accelerate the adaptation of workers to new technologies, which in turn leads to a reorganization of labor.

4. *Sustain and promote company exports.* Companies need and must develop offensive strategies to conquer foreign markets. Industrial sectors, especially those of small economies that are unaffected by

globalization, are now very few. Developing exports has become an inevitable priority for companies of small nations with already limited domestic markets wanting to survive in the global economy.

In this respect, government must increase the support of exports by helping firms find new markets and develop trade strategies in foreign markets, re-channeling exports toward promising markets, encouraging and facilitating small companies to open up to foreign markets and foreign competition, and facilitating the creation of professional associations to reach the critical mass in order to withstand such foreign competition.

The new challenge for governments, especially for those of small countries, is to create these conditions stated above which will allow entrepreneurial creativity to flourish (World Competitiveness Report 1993, p. 268–289). It is believed that small economies are quite capable of succeeding in this endeavor thanks to their flexibility, which enables them to adjust quickly and efficiently to constantly changing economic conditions.

*Proposition 8:* Nation size does matter when it comes to economic internationalization. Small open economies' macro-organizational strategies in the form of efficient economic environment, good infrastructure, support for the science and technology sectors, and promoting the exporting sector tend to be more effectively implemented than are their larger counterparts' strategies when forging the complementary government/firm relationship necessary for the XXI century.

### 3.2.3 Corporatism and Macro-compromises

Corporatism is defined by Williamson (1989) as follows:

> "The effective participation of labour unions (and organized business) in policy formulation and implementation across all sectors and those policy areas that are of central importance for the management of the economy" (p. 149).

In other words, corporatism refers to the process of interest intermediation which involves the negotiation of economic policies between state agencies and interest organizations from the social division of labor.

In regard to macroeconomic policies, small economies tend to exhibit a higher degree of economic stability, already proven by the small Nordic countries (i.e., Denmark, Finland, and Sweden), which leads to a belief that they enjoy a more efficient allocation of natural and created resources and a higher level of welfare thanks to enhanced economic performance.

The key to strong corporatism lies in the realm of functional interest intermediation through highly formalized labor unions in direct relation with the private and the public sector. Moreover, those countries—for the most part small ones—fortunate enough to have developed a somewhat efficient practice of interest intermediation with their multiple, overlapping, spontaneously formed, voluntaristically supported, and politically autonomous groups are likely to enjoy a higher degree of *macro-compromises.*

Indeed, the literature points out the existence of a close correlation between corporatism and the size of a nation[40]. Grant (1985, p. 7) writes: "Corporatism seems to have been most successful at the macro level in small countries, and it could be that the historical verdict on corporatism will be that it is a phenomenon of small countries in prosperous times."

Moreover, Williamson (1989, p. 150–151) summarizes and ranks[41] previous studies supporting the positive relationship between corporatism and nation size. He reveals that strong corporatism is exhibited only by small nations such as Austria, Denmark, Finland, Sweden, Switzerland, and the Netherlands; medium corporatism as well is shown only by other small countries (with the single exception of Germany); and weak corporatism is displayed by large countries such as Canada, France, Italy, the United States, and Great Britain.

Williamson (1989) concludes that nation size may not be the only key variable. There may be some other institutional characteristics of small economies, discussed previously, that allow for a more flexible, understanding, unified, and centralized macro-structure of interest groups assisting in macro-compromises.

Corporatism's major agenda is the determination of incomes and the integration of organized working class people in a capitalist society. Furthermore, corporatist arrangements seek to achieve a consensual framework in which durable, long-lasting relationships between government, trade unions, and private businesses can be encouraged (as in the "Scandinavian Model" for example).

The small Nordic countries' corporatism is based on considerable class compromise, parliamentary alliances, and consensus seeking allowing those nations to attain a more even distribution of income and allowing them to make fast responses to external shocks. This system operates by defining *a growth path of earnings*. The upper limit of this path is determined by the minimum level of profits required to guarantee that corporations carry on and pursue new investment opportunities. If wages rise above the upper bound, then investment and productivity growth (emphasized by the New Growth Theory) will fall against the interests of both workers and employers. Moreover, if the exchange rate is fixed, then it can act as the nominal anchor in the system which to keep wages and prices under control, thus maintaining international competitiveness[42].

Additionally, the Swedish social democratic commitment to full employment and solidaristic wage policies has rooted a strong consensual framework in which durable relationships among government, labor unions, and firms provide more egalitarian and stable economic growth within a flexible institutional system[43].

*Proposition 9:* Small open economies tend to have a higher degree of corporatism compared to their larger counterparts, yielding a more flexible, understanding, egalitarian, and centralized macro-structure of interest groups; therefore, allowing for greater consensus and effectiveness in macro-economic policy management.

## 3.3 SUMMARY

Economic growth and international competitiveness of small nations to some degree is a matter of globalization and institutional change and flexibility. This chapter first has looked at the small nations' specific approaches of globalization and has derived six basic propositions dealing with trade, specialization, direct overseas businesses, exchange rates, price stability, and economic integration.

The chapter has also examined the institutional flexibility characteristics of small nations and has put forth three basic propositions dealing with flexibility, public and private sector complementarity, and corporatism. These propositions will be tested in the next chapter.

[illegible]

[illegible]

[illegible]

[illegible]

CHAPTER 4

# Classification, Degree of Globalization, and Empirical Evidence

## The European Union

A fundamental discovery of recent times is that a small open economy can secure economic growth through exports and FDI, either by enlarging its limited domestic market or by existing within a larger market, usually established by some kind of economic integration. Since this study is concerned with the economic implications of small open economies, compared to their larger counterparts, the member nations of the European Union will be the focus of this study.

It is recognized that small economies within the EU do have more similarities than differences; thus, making this analysis a possible reference point for the comparable small open economies in Eastern Europe such as Estonia, Latvia, Lithuania, Slovakia, and Slovenia, as they join the global economy as new independent economic actors.

Section 4.1 provides a brief history of the European Union and examines its enlargement from six with three small nations, to fifteen with ten small countries. Section 4.2 gives a classification of the EU members into small and large open economies. Section 4.3 evaluates and tests the propositions derived from Chapter Three. Section 4.4 examines the empirical procedure, data, and method of estimation. Section 4.5 presents the empirical results. Finally, a summary will conclude the chapter.

## 4.1 A BRIEF HISTORY OF THE EUROPEAN UNION

In great part, one of the unrecorded elements in the creation of the European Economic Community (EEC), later the Economic Community (EC), and now the European Union (EU), was the principle of containment against future conflicts initiated by threatening countries and ideologies, in particular, Fascism in Germany and Communism in the Soviet Bloc. After World War II, a devastated Europe was committed to economic revival. A customs union was signed by the Benelux countries in 1947. The forerunner to the EEC was thus born as the Benelux Economic Union (all three nations, Belgium, the Netherlands, and Luxembourg, are small open economies) (Rosenberg 1994, p. 1–3).

The future model for regional economic integration evolved when the foreign ministers of six nations, the Benelux nations, Italy, France, and West Germany met at Messina in 1955 to discuss the proposals for further European cooperation to build on the success story of the Benelux Economic Union. The Six signed the Treaty of Rome in 1957, which established the goals and formal working rules providing the basic principles for European economic integration[44].

Denmark, Ireland[45], and Great Britain were added in 1973. Greece became a full member in 1981, with Portugal and Spain joining in 1986. And finally, Austria, Finland, and Sweden have just joined in 1995, thus providing a unified market of 15 nations (ten of them considered small open economies) and a total market of more than 370 million sophisticated consumers.

## 4.2 CLASSIFICATION OF EUROPEAN UNION NATIONS

For this study smallness refers to the compactedness of a nation in the domestic economic space with the attributes of a small domestic market, a small geographical area, and a small natural resource endowment. In order to measure the degree of smallness—compactedness of a nation—and to account for its domestic economic space depicted by the above characteristics, demographic, geographical, and economic factors will be utilized as proxies. These factors are population, geographic size, and export value of primary products and fuels.

Hence, the degree of smallness is basically determined by a composite measure of selected characteristics, which can be summarized in accordance with these three variables at the macroeconomic level:

MS = Market Size,
GC = Geographical Compactedness, and
RP = Resource Paucity.

To account for these attributes, the following variables are used:

1. MS: Market Size determined by the demographic factor of population measured in millions;
2. GC: Geographical Compactedness evaluated by the geographic factor of nation size measured in square kilometers, and
3. RP: Resource Paucity accounted for by the economic factor of the export value of primary commodities and fuels measured in millions of dollars.

Each of these three attributes are assigned values from 0 to 5, according to the parameters shown in Table 4–1. These values are then summed for each country. Thus an economy can have a minimum score of zero and a maximum score of 15. The higher the score, the higher the degree of smallness. The cut-off points for each variable were constructed subjectively based upon the literature found on the size of nations and an intuitive sense of what seems reasonable.

**Table 4–1. Measurement of Smallness**

| Population (millions) | Nation Size (sq Km.) | Resource ($ millions) | Points Points |
|---|---|---|---|
| 0-2.999 | 0-29,999 | 0-2,999 | 5 |
| 3-5.999 | 30-59,999 | 3,000-5,999 | 4 |
| 6-8.999 | 60-89,999 | 6,000-8,999 | 3 |
| 9-11.999 | 90-119,999 | 9,000-11,999 | 2 |
| 12-14.999 | 120-149,999 | 12,000-14,999 | 1 |
| 15-Above | 150-Above | 15,000-Above | 0 |

Based on Tables 4–1 and 4–2, the classification of small and large economies within the European Union is the following:

**Table 4–2. European Union Nations**

| Nation | Pop. | Size | Export | Points |
|---|---|---|---|---|
| Austria | 8.0 (3) | 83,835 (3) | 4,789 (4) | 10 |
| Belgium | 10.1 (2) | 30,540 (4) | 22,086 (0) | 6 |
| Britain | 58.2 (0) | 243,977 (0) | 34,140 (0) | 0 |
| Denmark | 5.2 (4) | 43,076 (4) | 13,341 (1) | 9 |
| Finland | 5.1 (4) | 337,113 (0) | 4,186 (4) | 8 |
| France | 58.0 (0) | 547,026 (0) | 50,480 (0) | 0 |
| Germany | 81.6 (0) | 356,755 (0) | 43,720 (0) | 0 |
| Greece | 10.5 (2) | 131,944 (1) | 4,580 (4) | 7 |
| Holland | 15.4 (0) | 40,844 (4) | 50,960 (0) | 4 |
| Ireland | 3.6 (4) | 70,282 (3) | 7,787 (3) | 10 |
| Italy | 58.1 (0) | 301,223 (0) | 19,390 (0) | 0 |
| Luxembourg | .4 (5) | 2,586 (5) | 1,544 (5) | 15 |
| Spain | 39.2 (0) | 504,782 (0) | 14,191 (1) | 1 |
| Sweden | 8.8 (3) | 449,964 (0) | 8,329 (3) | 6 |
| Portugal | 9.4 (2) | 92,082 (2) | 3,134 (4) | 8 |

*Source:* World Bank Tables (1994)(:Number calculated as a percentage of Belgium's export value of primary and fuel products

**Table 4–3. Classification of EU Nations**

| Small Economies | Large Economies |
|---|---|
| Luxembourg (15) | Spain (1) |
| Austria (10) | Britain (0) |
| Ireland (10) | France (0) |
| Denmark (9) | Germany (0) |
| Finland (8) | Italy (0) |
| Portugal (8) | |
| Greece (7) | |
| Belgium (6) | |
| Sweden (6) | |
| Holland (4) | |

A nation with a total score of 4 or more will be small considered a small country; therefore, any nation with a score of 3 or less will be considered a large country

As a reminder for the reader of the subjectivity of the concept of smallness, the cut-off point of 4 has been selected arbitrarily.

## 4.3 PROPOSITIONS EVALUATED

The framework as reviewed in Chapters Two and Three explains the reasons for the globalization of small economies to secure economic growth. Moreover, globalization does affect growth rates through its influence on factor accumulation and knowledge creation. Small open economies, which already need to compete in global markets to increase their limited domestic markets are also being forced to generate new ideas that are truly innovative on a global scale to create dynamic comparative advantages (emphasized by the New Growth Theory) in order to achieve economic growth. This section develops a link between globalization and economic growth and the empirical work in the next section.

### 4.3.1 Globalization to Overcome Smallness and Secure Economic Growth

As outlined in Chapter Three, the increased exchange of goods and knowledge has encouraged a growing interdependence among nations' technological advancement and long-term performances, in particular for small open economies.

Trade theory indicates that there are *static gains* from exploiting comparative advantage, but does not provide any basis for expecting open economies, especially small ones, to grow more rapidly over long periods of time. Globalization does affect growth rates of "less developed" European nations through its influence on factor accumulation, knowledge creation, and dynamic external economies.

The preceding analysis of the globalization strategies of small nations showed that compared to their counterparts, small economies, when they are economically successful, are (1) more export focused in manufacturing; (2) more specialized in differentiated manufactures, which provides the creation of dynamic comparative advantages, focusing on niche-market goods; (3) more actively involved with direct overseas businesses in order to expand small domestic markets and to exploit the market power attained through dynamic comparative advantage; (4) more sensitive in strategically managing exchange rates as a macroeconomic instrument of competitiveness for its firms; (5) likely to be in a better position to achieve price stability; and (6) more actively involved in international trade through varying degrees of economic integration, which facilitates the process of technological absorption and dissemination[46].

### 4.3.2 Testing Propositions

First of all to test whether a relationship exists between nation size and trade (see Proposition 1, p. 26), a comparison of the ratio of exports plus imports to total GNP for small and large economies within the European Union members will be made. In addition, *total GNP* will be regressed against *exports* for small and large nations as well. It is hypothesized that the relationships existing between the dependent and the independent variable are in both cases *positive*. But it is also postulated that the coefficient of exports for small countries will be greater than the coefficient of exports for their larger counterparts.

$$TGNP = a + bX_{export} + e; \quad b > 0 \text{ and } b_{small} > b_{large}$$

To test whether a second relationship exists between nation size and export manufactures in niche-markets (see Proposition 2, p. 26), the export manufactures to total GNP ratio for small and large economies in the EU will be compared, under the assumption that manufactured goods are the only products sold in the global niche-markets. Moreover, *total GNP* will be regressed against *manufactured exports* for small and large nations. It is also hypothesized that the relationship existing between the dependent and the independent variable is in both cases *positive*, but it is again postulated that the coefficient of export manufactures for small countries will be greater than the coefficient of export manufactures for large nations.

$$TGNP = a + bX_{man\ export} + e; \quad b > 0 \text{ and } b_{small} > b_{large}$$

This study has also proposed that small open economies tend to develop more direct business links, especially through FDI, than their larger counterparts. (see Proposition 3, p. 28). Ideally, if inward and outward FDI for each country were to be reported in international data surveys, the same procedure as in Propositions 1 and 2 would be used. However, there is no breakdown of these numbers for all EU members, but inward and outward FDI stock figures can still be used to compare the FDI to total GNP ratio for small and large nations. In addition, *total*

*GNP* against the *FDI* ratio (inward+outward/TGNP) will be regressed for small and large economies. Once again, it is hypothesized that the relationship existing between TGNP and FDI is in both cases *positive* and, it is theorized that the coefficient of FDI for small nations will be greater than the coefficient of FDI for larger ones.

$$TGNP = a + bX_{FDI} + e; \quad b > 0 \text{ and } b_{small} > b_{large}$$

Another important factor to be analyzed in this section is the strategic management of exchange rates. Obviously, what really matters for international competitiveness is not the nominal exchange rate but rather the real exchange rate. Hence, the hypothesis is that small open economies, as compared to their larger counterparts, are more likely to make their home currencies undervalued. Thus, the real exchange rate[47], R-the home currency price of \$, $(R = e\, p_i^d / p_{US})*100$ will be compared to the nominal exchange rate, e, between small and large nations. It should not be observed the same real depreciations in the large EU economies as in the small EU economies.

To test whether a relationship exists between nation size and price stability (see Proposition 5, p. 34), a simple comparison will be made between the inflation rates for small and large EU members.

Finally, to test whether a relationship exists between nation size and economic integration (see Proposition 6, p. 38), past history will be examined. The analysis will begin with the customs union agreement by the Benelux countries (three nations) in 1947, followed in 1957 with the Treaty of Rome (six countries), and concluding with the 1973, 1981, 1986, and 1995 European Union enlargements (15 nations)[48].

The same procedure will be used to test the propositions examined in Section 3.2, using survey data from the "World Competitiveness Report" (1992, 1993, 1994).

The next test is to determine whether a relationship exists between nation size and flexibility (see Proposition 7, p. 39). The degree to which the governments of small and large EU economies display flexibility and effectiveness in adapting their economic policies to a changing international environment will be determined. It is hypothesized that the means of the two groups are not equal and are therefore statistically significant.

Another important factor to be analyzed in this section is whether a second relationship exists between nation size and macro-organizational strategies (see proposition 8, p. 43). To determine this degree of small and large country governments' interference that is considered positive and encourages the development of businesses will be measured. Again, it is hypothesized that the means of the country groupings are not equal.

Finally to test whether a relationship exists between nation size and corporatism (see Proposition 9, p. 45), the ratings on government policies that are supported by public consensus among the small and large members of the EU will be compared. It is postulated that the small and large country groups exhibit a difference in means that is statistically significant.

## 4.4 EMPIRICAL PROCEDURES[49]

### 4.4.1 Data and Method of Estimation[50]

The data used to test the propositions was obtained from the following sources: *World Tables 1994*, (a World Bank publication), *International Financial Statistics 1993 & 1994*, (an International Monetary Fund publication), *World Competitiveness Report 1992, 1993 & 1994*, (a World Economic Forum, and IMD publication), and *World Investment Report 1994*, (a United Nations publication).

Data collection presents a special problem when attempting to empirically test the institutional propositions, since *The World Competitiveness Report* has changed the data collection format on several occasions. In addition, the early issues are very difficult to find. In contrast, testing the globalization propositions is less troublesome due to the availability of good data in the *World Tables*, the *International Financial Statistics*, and the *World Investment Report*.

Estimation of economic relationships among small and large economies (cross-section data) that are observed at more than one point in time (time series data) is a problem. The main difficulty lies in determining how to specify a statistical model that will capture country differences in behavior.

A large number of observations is desirable for testing any model. The "pooling" technique is widely used in order to achieve higher degrees of freedom. Thus, cross-section (countries) and time-series (years; 1973–1992) will be pooled to secure sufficient degrees of freedom and efficient parameters. Combining cross-section and time-series data creates difficulty since the disturbance term might consist of time-series related disturbances, cross-section disturbances or a combination of the two.

Because the only objective of this analysis is to show that there is a positive correlation between these variables and that small economies exhibit larger coefficients than their larger counterparts, a General Linear Model[51] (GLM) technique, in which pooled data uses dummy variables will be employed. This method specifies that only the intercept parameter varies across countries. It also provides a more compact 'X-matrix' than other methods.

The coefficients are specified as follows: (small country; i = 1, . . ., N = 10), (large country; j = 1, . . ., N = 5), (time; t = 1, . . ., T = 20, if EU member since 1973):

$$
\begin{array}{ccc}
b_{1it} = b_{1i} & & b_{1jt} = b_{1j} \\
\vdots & \text{and} & \vdots \\
b_{10it} = b_{10i} & & b_{5jt} = b_{5j}
\end{array}
$$

This model of parameter variation specifies that *only* the *intercept* parameter varies, and the intercept varies only *across* countries and not over time. Thus, it can be said that *all behavioral differences between individual countries and over time are captured by the intercept.* The resulting regression model is:

$$y_{it} = b_{1i} + b_2 X_{2it} + e_{it}$$

This regression is more conventionally written by defining dummy variables for each country; for example,

$$
\begin{array}{lcl}
D_{1i} = \begin{cases} 1, & i = 1 \\ 0, & \text{otherwise} \end{cases} & & D_{1j} = \begin{cases} 1, & j = 1 \\ 0, & \text{otherwise} \end{cases} \\
\vdots & \text{and} & \vdots \\
D_{10i} = \begin{cases} 1, & i = 10 \\ 0, & \text{otherwise} \end{cases} & & D_{5j} = \begin{cases} 1, & j = 5 \\ 0, & \text{otherwise} \end{cases}
\end{array}
$$

Then, under this specification of dummy variables, the linear regression model for the seven small open economies becomes:

$$y_{it} = b_{1,1} D_{1i} + b_{1,2} D_{2i} + \ldots + b_{1,10} D_{10i} + b_2 X_{2it} + e_{it}$$

The linear statistical model for the five large economies becomes:

$$y_{jt} = b_{1,1} D_{1j} + b_{1,2} D_{2j} + \ldots + b_{1,5} D_{5j} + b_2 X_{2jt} + e_{jt}$$

Based on the regressions above, small versus large open economies within the European Union boundaries since 1973 to 1992 will be compared[52]. However, Ireland will have 20 observations (1973–1992), but Spain will have only 7 observations (1986–1992), since it joined the EU in 1986.

### 4.4.2 Tests Performed on the Statistical Analysis

*T-Test*

This test computes a t-statistic for testing the hypothesis that the means of two groups of observations are equal. It computes the t-statistic based on the assumption that the variances of the two groups are equal. It also assumes that the variables are normally and independent distributed within each group[53].

*Cochran Test*

This test uses the Cochran and Cox approximation of the probability level of the estimated t-statistics to take into account the unequal variance situation.

## 4.5 EMPIRICAL RESULTS

There are two primary issues being analyzed globalization and institutional strategies of small economies within the European Union[54]. The following sections will look at each proposition by first comparing their statistical significance among small and large nations, then appraising new economic phenomenon, and finally, regressing total GNP to different export data.

This is done to capture the fundamental concept that the size of a nation *does matter* in the internationalization and institutional process, especially for small economies. The results of the statistical testing are summarized in the Appendix of this chapter.

### 4.5.1 Globalization Propositions

*Proposition One (Trade Focus).* It is evident that smaller economies have a higher trade ratio (exports plus imports to total GNP) as compared to large economies. A t-test was used to examine the hypothesis that the means of the two groups of observations are equal. The mean of small nations' trade ratio is .87, more than double that of large countries' trade ratio of .37, and these results were statistically significant[55]. Moreover, the predicted positive relationship between the

**Figure 4–1. Trade (export-import) Focus**

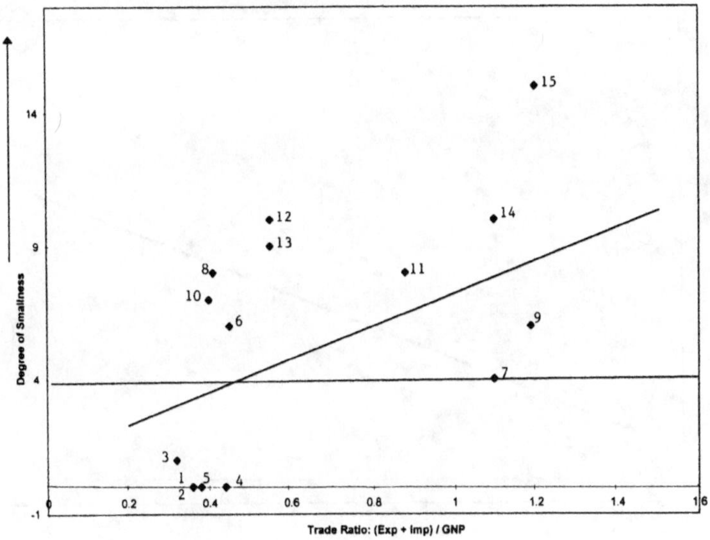


*Note:* Data extracted from the World Bank Tables (1994) from 1973 to 1992. The graph depicts the averages of the countries' trade ratios for the 1973–1992 period.

| Countries: | 1.France | 6.Sweden | 11.Portugal |
|---|---|---|---|
| | 2.Italy | 7.Holland | 12.Austria |
| | 3.Spain | 8.Finland | 13.Denmark |
| | 4.Britain | 9.Belgium | 14.Ireland |
| | 5.Germany | 10.Greece | 15.Luxembourg |

trade ratios of small and large nations was found to exist and is shown in Figure 4–1. Thus, nation size seems to matter when it comes to trade (see Appendix 4–1 and 4–2).

*Proposition Two (Specialization in niche market goods).* Small open economies have a higher ratio of manufactures trade (export manufactures to total GNP) than their larger counterparts. Again, the same technique as above was used to test the hypothesis that the means of the two groups of observations are equal. The mean of small nations' export manufactures ratio is .27, almost double that of the large coun

**Figure 4–2. "Niche-Market" Goods Specialization**

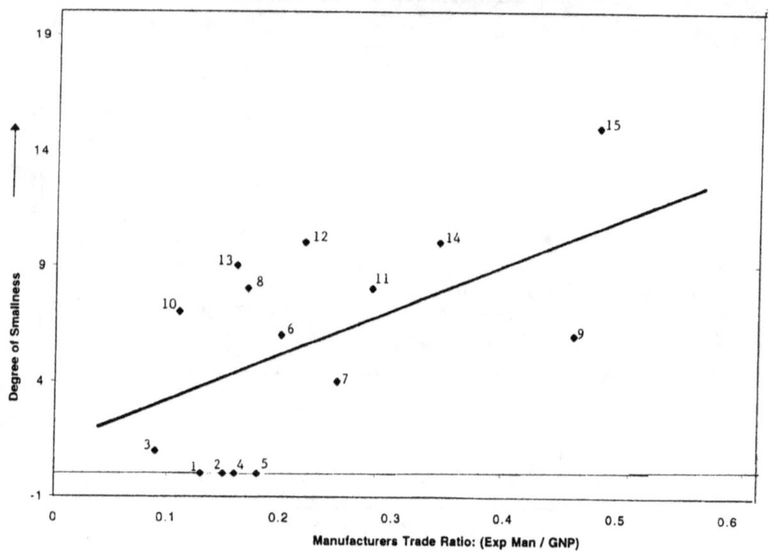


*Note:* Data obtained from the World Bank Tables (1994) from 1973 to 1992. The graph illustrates the averages of the nations' trade manufactures ratios for the 1973–1992 period.

| Countries: | 1.France | 6.Sweden | 11.Portugal |
|---|---|---|---|
| | 2.Italy | 7.Holland | 12.Austria |
| | 3.Spain | 8.Finland | 13.Denmark |
| | 4.Britain | 9.Belgium | 14.Ireland |
| | 5.Germany | 10.Greece | 15.Luxembourg |

tries' ratio of .14, and these results were statistically significant. Moreover, the predicted positive relationship between the export manufactures ratios of small and large nations was found to exist and is shown in Figure 4–2. Thus, nation size appears to matter when it comes to the concentration of manufactured products in world niche-markets (see Appendix 4–1 and 4–2).

*Proposition Three (Involvement in direct overseas businesses).* Big MNCs from small economies have greater direct business links, especially in FDI, than their larger counterparts. Once again, a t-test was used to examine the hypothesis that the means of the two groups of observations are equal. The mean of small countries' inward-FDI ratio is .129, higher than that of large nations' inward-FDI which is .091. Moreover, the mean of small countries' outward-FDI ratio is .13, again higher than that of large nations' outward-FDI of .088, but these results were not statistically significant[56]. However, the predicted positive relationship between the inward and outward FDI ratios of small and large economies was found to exist and is shown in Figures 4–3A and 4–3B. Thus, nation size seems to matter in international business links, especially in FDI (see Appendix 4–1 and 4–2).

**Figure 4–3A. International Business: Inward FDI Focus**

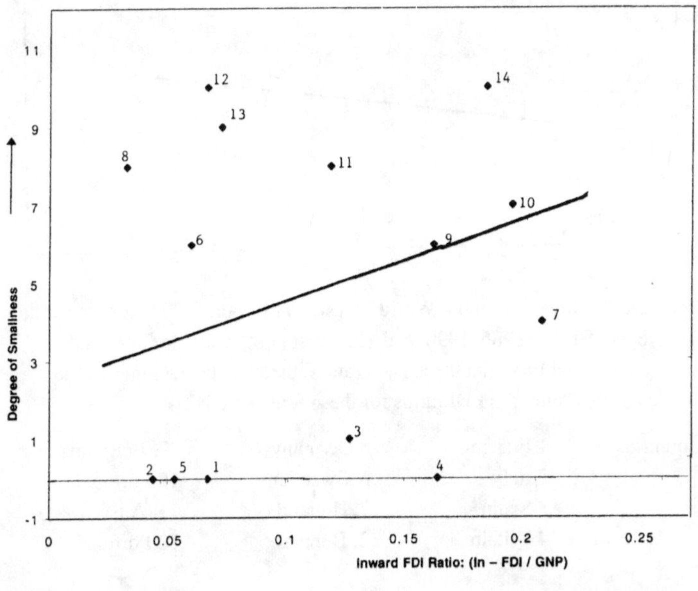

*Note:* Data extracted from the World Investment Report (1994) for the available years of 1980, 1985, 1990, and 1992 (data not available for Luxembourg). The graph depicts the averages of the countries' inward FDI ratios for these four periods.

| Countries: | 1.France | 6.Sweden | 11.Portugal |
|---|---|---|---|
| | 2.Italy | 7.Holland | 12.Austria |
| | 3.Spain | 8.Finland | 13.Denmark |
| | 4.Britain | 9.Belgium | 14.Ireland |
| | 5.Germany | 10.Greece | |

**Figure 4–3B. International Business: Outward FDI Focus**

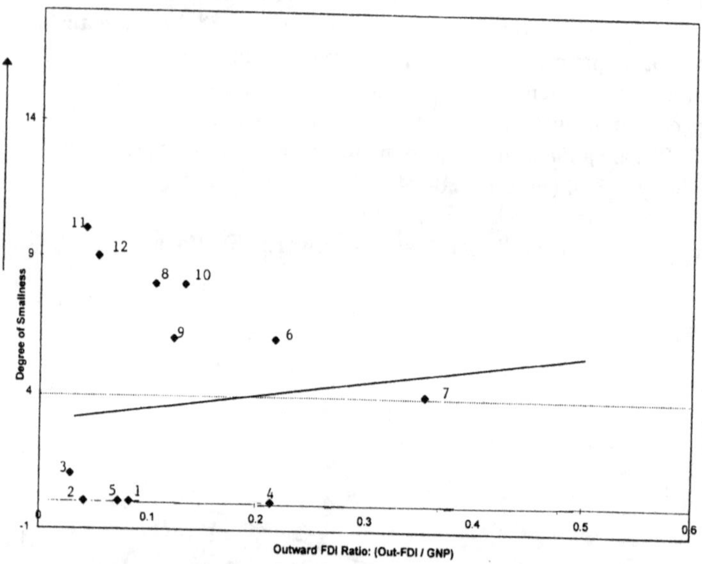


*Note:* Data obtained from the World Investment Report (1994) for the available years of 1980, 1985, 1990, and 1992 (data not available for Greece, Ireland, and Luxembourg). The graph illustrates the averages of the countries' outward FDI ratios for these four periods.

| Countries: | 1.France | 5.Germany | 9. Belgium |
|---|---|---|---|
| | 2.Italy | 6. Sweeden | 10 Portugal |
| | 3.Spain | 7. Holland | 11. Austria |
| | 4.Britain | 12. Denmark | 10.Portugal |

*Proposition Four (Strategic management and use of exchange rates).* Small open economies manage their exchange rates as an instrument of competitiveness due to their heavy dependence on trade. They attempt to price their exports competitively through exchange rate management.

Small nations' changes in the real exchange rate were of large magnitude during the 1973–1992 period. For example, the nominal exchange rate for Ireland depreciated by 29.86 percent, but its real exchange rate depreciated by 59.20 percent; despite the nominal rate appreciation of .5 percent for Denmark, its real rate depreciated as much as 17.46 percent; and for Portugal, the nominal rate depreciated by 82.40 percent, but the real rate depreciated even further by 97.87 percent.

In contrast, large nations' changes in the real exchange rates were also of considerable magnitude. For example, the nominal exchange rate for France depreciated by 14.50 percent, but its real exchange rate depreciated by 38.60 percent; and for Spain and Italy, their nominal exchange rate depreciated by 50.31 and 58.80 percent respectively, but their real exchange rate depreciated by over 80 percent[57] (see Appendix 4–3).

Furthermore, from the period of 1979 to 1992, the prediction of smaller nations' necessity of larger real depreciations to weather the second oil shock of 1979 was found to exist with the exception of Holland and Austria, both of which were heavily trade dependent on Germany. Holland, Austria, and Germany actually experienced nominal, and even greater, real appreciation of their currencies.

The rest of the small European Union members did experience larger real depreciations than their larger counterparts. For example, Belgium, Luxembourg, Denmark, Ireland, Sweden, Finland, Portugal, and Greece, experienced nominal depreciations ranging from around 14 to 80 percent; but the real rates varied from around 10 percent to over 95 percent.

Larger nations' nominal depreciations ranged from 27 to 45 percent and the real rates fluctuated from 39 to almost 67 percent, considerably less than their smaller counterparts (see Table 4–4).

*Proposition Five (Price stability).* Small open economies, under a *truly* flexible exchange rate, tend to better manage inflationary pressures than their larger counterparts. In the case of the European Union, the somewhat *fixed* exchange rate does complicate the analysis.

**Table 4–4. Strategic Management of Exchange Rates:1979–92**

| Nation | Nominal Exchange Rate | Real Exchange Rate |
|---|---|---|
| Small | | |
| Austria | + 9.50 | + 19.43 |
| Belgium | - 15.47 | - 9.34 |
| Denmark | - 14.24 | - 20.94 |
| Finland | - 29.25 | - 42.0 |
| Greece | - 82.20 | - 96.24 |
| Holland | + 5.0 | + 39.35 |
| Ireland | - 24.0 | - 39.10 |
| Luxembourg | - 15.47 | - 16.60 |
| Sweden | - 41.10 | - 58.10 |
| Portugal | - 66.10 | - 92.37 |
| Large | | |
| Britain | - 32.05 | - 49.10 |
| Germany | + 7.30 | + 29.95 |
| France | - 27.0 | - 39.12 |
| Italy | - 45.24 | - 72.90 |
| Spain | - 42.30 | - 66.98 |

*Source:* International Financial Statistics (1993 & 1994).

Since control of the money supply and strategic management of exchange rates within the EU is very limited, it appears that inflation rates in Western Europe are clustered fairly close together. The inflation rates for both small and large economies were a little over 8 percent[58].

The predicted positive relationship between inflation rates of small and large nation in the Western European countries was not found to exist. This relationship is shown in Figure 4–4. This is not surprising with increasing monetary integration in the European Union (see Appendix 4–4 and 4–5).

**Figure 4-4 Price Stability and Inflation**

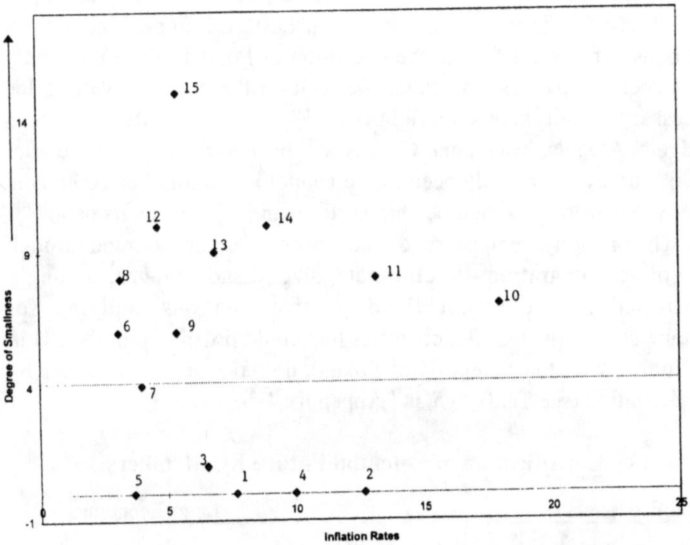


*Note:* Data extracted from the World Bank Tables (1994) from 1973 to 1992. The graph depicts the average of the nations' inflation rates for the 1973–1992 period.

| *Countries:* | | | |
|---|---|---|---|
| | 1.France | 6.Sweden | 11.Portugal |
| | 2.Italy | 7.Holland | 12.Austria |
| | 3.Spain | 8.Finland | 13.Denmark |
| | 4.Britain | 9.Belgium | 14.Ireland |
| | 5.Germany | 10.Greece | 15.Luxembourg |

*Proposition Six (International economic integration).* Small open economies engage in trade through varying degrees of economic integration to eliminate size disadvantages. The first attempt at economic integration in Europe began with the Benelux Economic Union, formed by three small nations in 1947. Almost fifty years later, the European Union has fifteen members, ten considered small economies. Recently the 1995 European Union enlargement included three new small countries, Austria, Finland, and Sweden.

Fifteen more countries are in line as actual or potential candidates for membership of the Union, and all except one are small open economies. Of the EU's associates from Eastern Europe, nine nations are considered small[59] with the exception of Poland. As of now, only the Czechs, Slovenes, and Poles are well on the way to fulfilling the necessary requirements for admission[60]. The three Mediterranean midgets, Albania, Malta, and Cyprus will have to wait some time after 1996. Turkey has already been told it cannot join until after 2000. And finally, Switzerland's membership is still being rejected by its people[61].

Thus nation size appears to matter when it comes to trade through economic integration to eliminate size disadvantages, strongly confirmed by the recent flood of small nations applying for membership to the EU. All countries that could possibly join the EU in the future, with the exception of Poland, do have small economies by our definition (see Table 4–5 and Appendix 4–6).

**Table 4–5. Classification of Potential Future EU Members**

| Small Economies | Large Economies |
|---|---|
| Malta (15) | |
| Cyprus (15) | Poland (3) |
| Switzerland (11) | |
| Slovenia (10) | |
| Albania (9) | |
| Estonia (9) | |
| Hungary (8) | |
| Slovakia (8) | |
| Latvia (8) | |
| Lithuania (7) | |
| Czech Republic (5) | |
| Bulgaria (5) | |
| Romania (5) | |
| Turkey (4) | |

### 4.5.2 Institutional Propositions

*Proposition Seven (Flexibility).* Small nations *must* be flexible to endure the rapidly changing economic conditions of the 1990's and to continue to quickly adjust to future external shocks. A nation's flexibility was measured from the results of the 1992, 1993, and 1994 Executive Opinion Survey question: do government adapt economic policies to new economic realities effectively?

A t-test was used to examine the hypothesis that the means of the two groups of observations are equal. The mean of small nations' flexibility is 5.02, which is considerably higher than the larger nations'

**Figure 4–5. Flexibility and Adaptive Focus**

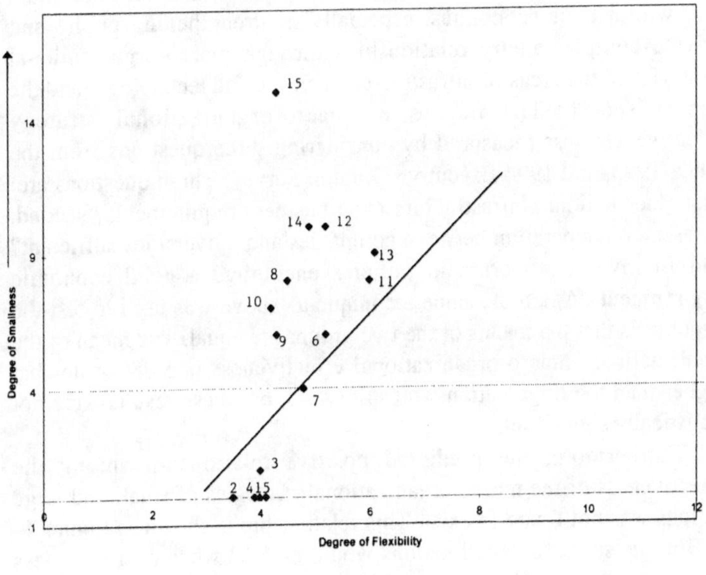


*Note:* Data extracted from the World Competitiveness Report (1992, 1993, and 1994). The graphs depicts the averages of the nations' adaptability and flexibility focus for the early 1990's.

| Countries: | 1.France | 6.Sweden | 11.Portugal |
|---|---|---|---|
| | 2.Italy | 7.Holland | 12.Austria |
| | 3.Spain | 8.Finland | 13.Denmark |
| | 4.Britain | 9.Belgium | 14.Ireland |
| | 5.Germany | 10.Greece | 15.Luxembourg |

mean of 3.88, and these results were statistically significant. These numbers represent the average of the Executive Opinion Scoreboard's results for the 1992–1994 period[62].

Furthermore, the predicted positive relationship among the degrees of flexibility of small and large nations was found to exist and is shown in Figure 4–5. Thus, nation size appears to matter when it comes to flexibility and adaptability (see Appendix 4–7 and 4–8).

*Proposition Eight (Government-Firm complementary relationship).* Governments of small countries do play a very important role within their economies, especially in strengthening public and private complementary relationships through macro-organizational strategies in the areas of infrastructure, science and technology, and the export sector. The degree of macro-organizational strategy effectiveness was measured by considering three questions from the 1992, 1993, and 1994 Executive Opinion Survey. These questions are: first, does national infrastructure meet business requirements? second, is research cooperation between companies and universities sufficient? and finally, do government policies encourage a good economic environment? Again the same technique as above was used to test the hypothesis that the means of the two groups are equal. The mean of the small nations' macro-organizational effectiveness is 5.08, somewhat higher than the large nations' mean of 4.43, but these results were not statistically significant.

Furthermore, the predicted positive relationship among the effectiveness of the macro-organizational strategies of small and large nations was not found to exist. This relationship is shown in Figure 4–6. But, the score for small nations would be 5.52 when excluding less developed countries like Portugal and Greece. Then, the predicted statistical significance would be found assuming equal variances in both groups. Thus, nation size appears to matter somewhat in the effectiveness of these macro-organizational strategies (see Appendix 4–7 and 4–8).

**Figure 4–6. Macro-Organizational Strategic Behavior**

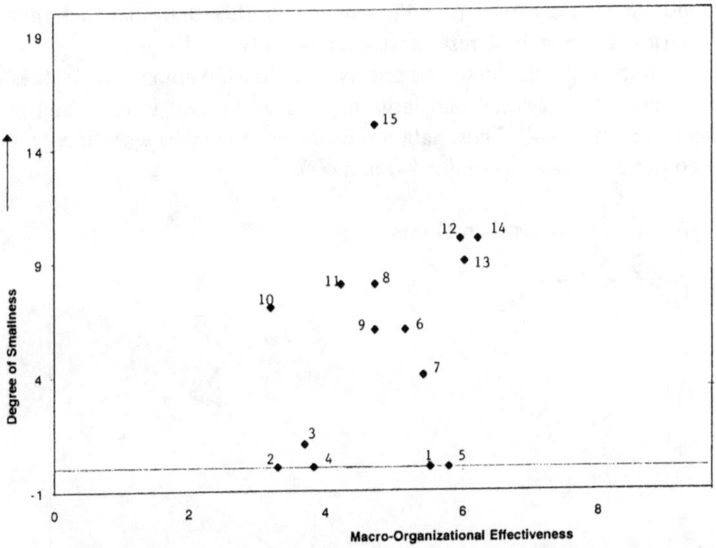


*Note:* Data obtained from the World Competitiveness Report (1992, 1993, and 1994). The graph depicts the averages of the nations' macro-organizational strategies effectiveness for the early 1990's.

| Countries: | 1.France | 6.Sweden | 11.Portugal |
|---|---|---|---|
| | 2.Italy | 7.Holland | 12.Austria |
| | 3.Spain | 8.Finland | 13.Denmark |
| | 4.Britain | 9.Belgium | 14.Ireland |
| | 5.Germany | 10.Greece | 15.Luxembourg |

*Proposition Nine (Corporatism).* Small countries show a strong degree of corporatism with regard to macroeconomic policy management dealing with wage differentials and the working class and, most importantly, yielding a more egalitarian and centralized macro-structure of interest groups. The degree of corporatism was measured by simply looking at the 1992, 1993, and 1994 Executive Opinion Survey question: are government policies supported by public consensus?

Again the same technique as before was used to test the hypothesis that the means of the two groups are equal. The mean of small economies' corporatism is 5.48, which is higher than that of larger countries, 4.0, and these results were statistically significant.

Additionally, the predicted positive relationship among the degrees of corporatism of small and large nations was found to exist and is shown in Figure 4–7. Thus, nation size appears to matter when it comes to corporatism (see Appendix 4–7 and 4–8).

**Figure 4–7. Corporatism Focus**

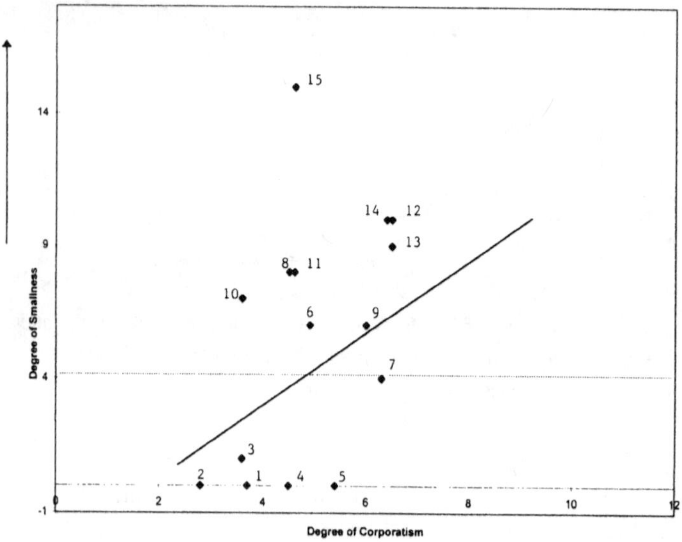


*Note:* Data obtained from the World Competitiveness Report (1992, 1993, and 1994). The graph depicts the averages of the countries' corporatism focus for the early 1990's.

| Countries: | 1.France | 6.Sweden | 11.Portugal |
|---|---|---|---|
| | 2.Italy | 7.Holland | 12.Austria |
| | 3.Spain | 8.Finland | 13.Denmark |
| | 4.Britain | 9.Belgium | 14.Ireland |
| | 5.Germany | 10.Greece | 15.Luxembourg |

### 4.5.3 Regression Analysis

Due to the importance of exports and FDI as the main engines of economic growth for small open economies, GNP is regressed on exports, export manufactures, and FDI. A cross country sample is used, thus forcing a pooling of the data across small and large open economies.
Hence;

1. GNP = f(exports),
2. GNP = f(export manufactures), and
3. GNP = f(FDI)

As with any linear regression exercise, the results should be interpreted with caution since important variables may not be fully captured.

Exports, export manufactures, and FDI in small open economies appear to be very important explaining changes in GNP. The small country coefficient estimates are all higher for exports, .16, export manufactures, .21, and FDI, .08 in small nations, than for their larger counterparts of .066, .074, and .05 respectively, revealing the significance of trade and FDI in small economies. Higher levels of trade and FDI help to overcome smallness and to secure economic growth. All regressions exhibit $R^2$s of .79 or higher. These results substantiate those obtained previously while testing the globalization propositions (see Table 4–6).

**Table 4–6. Trade, Trade Manufactures, and FDI**

| Nation | Coeficient Estimates(t stat) | R-Square |
|---|---|---|
| Small | | |
| Export | .16173 (14.25) | .81634 |
| Exman | .20772 (13.01) | .79257 |
| FDI | .08525 (3.70) | .79737 |
| Large | | |
| Export | .06624 (20.78) | .85830 |
| Exman | .07380 (18.80) | .83270 |
| FDI | .04848 (7.52) | .85096 |

## 4.6 SUMMARY

The first part of the chapter provided a brief history of the European Union, and a small versus large classification of its member-nations. The latter part of the chapter has been devoted to testing and presenting the empirical results of the globalization and institutional propositions derived from Chapter Three.

The results present evidence to support the concept that nation size does matter in international trade, especially in the globalization efforts of small economies, compared to their larger counterparts.

Although precise data are not available, the results seem to present enough evidence to advocate the idea that nation size does matter when dealing with economic flexibility and institutional characteristics of small countries compared to their larger counterparts.

**Appendix 4–1. Trade, Trade Manufactures, and FDI Ratios to GNP, 1973–1992**

| Nation | Trade Ratio | Trade Manufactures Ratio | FDI Ratio |
|---|---|---|---|
| Austria | .55 | .22 | .11 |
| Belgium | 1.20 | .45 | .29 |
| Denmark | .55 | .16 | .12 |
| Finland | .40 | .17 | .14 |
| Greece | .41 | .11 | .14 |
| Holland | 1.10 | .25 | .56 |
| Ireland | 1.08 | .34 | .18 |
| Luxembourg | 1.20 | .47 | N/A |
| Portugal | .88 | .28 | .14 |
| Sweden | .45 | .20 | .28 |
| Britain | .44 | .16 | .38 |
| France | .36 | .13 | .15 |
| Germany | .38 | .18 | .13 |
| Italy | .36 | .15 | .09 |
| Spain | .32 | .09 | .16 |

*Source:* World Bank Tables and World Investment Report (1994)

## Appendix 4–2 Trade, Trade Manufactures, and FDI Focus: 1973–1992[63]

| | Univariate Procedure | | |
|---|---|---|---|
| | Mean (%) | Variance | Std. Dev. |
| Trade Focus | | | |
| Nation | | | |
| Small | .87 | .103 | .32 |
| Large | .37 | .002 | .04 |
| Trade Manuf. Focus | | | |
| Nation | | | |
| Small | .27 | .0155 | .12 |
| Large | .14 | .001 | .032 |
| FDI Focus | | | |
| Nation | | | |
| Small | .22 | 208.85 | 14.45 |
| Large | .18 | 130.67 | 11.43 |

| | T-Test Procedure | |
|---|---|---|
| | T Prob> | T |
| Trade Focus | | |
| Variances | | |
| Unequal | -3.75 | .013 |
| Equal | -3.40 | .008 |
| F' | 60.81 | .0015 |
| Trade Manuf. Focus | | |
| Variances | | |
| Unequal | -2.33 | .068 |
| Equal | -2.14 | .0612 |
| F' | 15.54 | .020 |
| FdI Focus | | |
| Variances | | |
| Unequal | -.54 | .59 |
| Equal | -.51 | .62 |
| F' | 1.60 | .68 |

## Appendix 4–3. Strategic Management of Exchange Rates: 1973–1992

| Nation | Nominal Exchange Rate | Real Exchange Rate |
|---|---|---|
| Austria | + 74.83 | + 113.40 |
| Belgium | + 24.53 | + 33.97 |
| Denmark | + .5 | - 17.46 |
| Finland | - 26.70 | - 53.20 |
| Greece | - 86.16 | - 98.0 |
| Holland | +55.69 | + 115.16 |
| Ireland | - 29.86 | - 59.20 |
| Luxembourg | + 24.53 | + 33.26 |
| Portugal | - 82.40 | - 97.87 |
| Sweden | - 34.86 | - 59.84 |
| Britain | - 34.92 | - 68.20 |
| France | - 14.50 | - 38.60 |
| Germany | + 24.97 | + 145.0 |
| Italy | - 58.70 | - 87.30 |
| Spain | - 50.31 | - 83.42 |

*Source:*International Financial Statistics (1993 & 1994)

## Appendix 4–4. Price Stability-Inflation Rates[64]: 1973–1992

| | | Univariate Procedure | |
|---|---|---|---|
| Nation | Mean (%) | Variance | Std. Dev. |
| Belgium | 5.41 | 8.60 | 2.93 |
| Denmark | 6.93 | 11.92 | 3.45 |
| Greece | 17.99 | 11.85 | 3.44 |
| Holland | 4.03 | 9.99 | 3.16 |
| Ireland | 9.03 | 45.59 | 6.75 |
| Luxembourg | 5.48 | 19.30 | 4.39 |
| Portugal | 13.17 | 1.27 | 1.13 |
| Britain | 10.0 | 39.36 | 6.27 |
| France | 7.70 | 14.92 | 3.86 |
| Germany | 3.67 | 1.91 | 1.38 |
| Italy | 12.67 | 30.23 | 5.50 |
| Spain | 6.58 | .48 | .70 |

**Appendix 4–5. Inflation Rates Convergence: 1973–92**

| | Mean (%) | Univariate Procedure<br>Variance | Std. Dev. |
|---|---|---|---|
| Nation | | | |
| Small | 8.86 | 25.49 | 5.04 |
| Large | 8.12 | 1.65 | 3.41 |

| | T Prob > | T-Test Procedure<br>T |
|---|---|---|
| Variances | | |
| Unequal' | - .3024 | .7745 |
| Equal | - .2825 | .7833 |
| F | 2.19 | .4684 |

**Appendix 4–6. Economic Integration: Future EU members**

| Nation | Pop. | Size | Export | Points |
|---|---|---|---|---|
| Cyprus | .72 (5) | 9,251 (5) | 212 (5) | 15 |
| Malta | .36 (5) | 316 (5) | 68 (5) | 15 |
| Switzerl. | 6.90 (3) | 41,228 (4) | 4,154 (4) | 11 |
| Turkey | 58.54 (0) | 780,576 (0) | 4,208 (4) | 4 |
| Poland | 38.36 (0) | 312,612 (0) | 6,060 (3) | 3 |
| Czech Rep. | 10.36 (2) | 78,864 (3) | N/A | 5 |
| Slovakia | 5.29 (4) | 49,035 (4) | N/A | 8 |
| Hungary | 10.31 (2) | 92,980 (2) | 3,665 (4) | 8 |
| Estonia | 1.55 (5) | 45,100 (4) | N/A | 9 |
| Latvia | 2.64 (5) | 64,600 (3) | N/A | 8 |
| Lithuania | 3.76 (4) | 65,200 (3) | N/A | 7 |
| Slovenia | 2.02 (5) | 20,256 (5) | N/A | 10 |
| Bulgaria | 8.50 (3) | 110,912 (0) | N/A | 5 |
| Romania | 22.75 (0) | 237,499 (0) | 1,047 (5) | 5 |
| Albania | 3.25 (4) | 28,748 (5) | N/A | 9 |

*Source:* World Bank Tables (1994)

**Appendix 4–7. Flexibility, Macro-Organizational, and Corporatism Ratings**

| Nation | Flexibility | Macro-Organizational | Corporatism |
|---|---|---|---|
| Austria | 5.2 | 5.97 | 6.5 |
| Belgium | 4.3 | 4.73 | 4.6 |
| Denmark | 6.1 | 6.23 | 6.5 |
| Finland | 4.2 | 4.73 | 4.5 |
| Greece | 4.5 | 3.20 | 3.6 |
| Holland | 4.8 | 5.43 | 6.3 |
| Ireland | 4.9 | 6.03 | 6.4 |
| Luxembourg | 4.3 | 4.73 | 4.6 |
| Portugal | 6.0 | 4.23 | 6.0 |
| Sweden | 5.2 | 5.17 | 4.9 |
| Britain | 3.9 | 3.83 | 4.5 |
| France | 4.0 | 5.53 | 3.7 |
| Germany | 4.1 | 5.80 | 5.4 |
| Italy | 3.5 | 3.30 | 2.8 |
| Spain | 3.9 | 3.70 | 3.6 |

*Source:* World Competitiveness Report (1992,93 & 94)

**Appendix 4–8. Flexibility, Macro-Organizational, and Corporatism Focus**

| | Univariate Procedure | | |
|---|---|---|---|
| | Mean | Variance | Std. Dev. |
| Flexibility | | | |
| Nation | | | |
| Small | 5.02 | .46 | .68 |
| Large | 3.88 | .05 | .23 |
| Macro-Organizational Strategy | | | |
| Nation | | | |
| Small | 5.08 | .96 | .98 |
| Large4 | .43 | 1.31 | 1.15 |
| Corporatism | | | |
| Nation | | | |
| Small | 5.48 | 1.18 | 1.09 |
| Large | 4.0 | .97 | .99 |

**Appendix 4–8.** *(continued)*

| | T-Test Procedure | |
|---|---|---|
| | T Prob > | T |
| Flexibility | | |
| Variances | | |
| Unequal | -4.59 | .003 |
| Equal | -3.58 | .004 |
| F' | 8.93 | .05 |
| Macro-Organizational Strategy | | |
| Variance | | |
| Unequal | -1.07 | .34 |
| Equal | -1.12 | .28 |
| F' | 1.37 | .65 |
| Corporatism | | |
| Variances | | |
| Unequal | -2.58 | .05 |
| Equal | -2.51 | .03 |
| F' | 1.21 | .91 |

CHAPTER 5

# Region and Country Case Studies

## Catalonia and New Zealand

This chapter includes both a regional and a country case study. The regional case study will be on Catalonia in Spain. This region has the attributes of a small open economy. Barcelona, the Mediterranean city and capital of an independent Catalonia during the Middle Ages and in brief periods afterward, was suppressed by the Franco dictatorship during forty years, with the Catalan language and traditions silenced and the regional government disbanded.

Now, with democracy and considerable autonomy restored, Catalonia still remains part of Spain but looks to Europe and the rest of the world for its economic future. Thus, Barcelona, the capital of Catalonia, may develop to be a powerful player within the European Union in the near future.

The country case study will be on New Zealand, a small open economy, which has demonstrated the success of more than ten years of economic restructuring by generating a budget surplus and growth rate of 5.3% in 1994[65]. New Zealand is becoming an economic prototype for future reference by other small open economies.

The "Kiwi School of Economics" advocates that all a country needs is the *right policies*. The OECD predicts a continuous growth rate of 4% for the next couple of years. "Nowadays the problem is not a shortage of jobs but a shortage of skilled New Zealanders to fill them. . . . Ten years ago, this little Prometheus unchained itself from a rock of high taxes, high tariffs, heavy welfare burdens and pro-union labor laws. Now the economy is responding just as the textbooks say-like a smoothly self-adjusting growth machine.[66]"

Section 5.1 is devoted to the presentation of the region case study of Catalonia, and Section 5.2 presents the country case study of New Zealand. Finally, a summary concludes the chapter.

## 5.1 CATALONIA: A REGION CASE STUDY

The name Catalonia has a certain recognition among Southern European regions. The region has two distinctive characteristics: first, Barcelona, the capital, belongs to the select club of great cosmopolitan Mediterranean cities which have managed to retain a human scale. Yet it is more than an individual city like Marseilles, or Naples, for it is the capital of Catalonia, whose citizens share a common language (Catalan) and a common culture. Furthermore, within this small region there is great variety. There is a major mountain range (the Pyrenees) with many subsidiary spurs and protuberances, but there is also a seacoast of 580 kilometers in length and expanding, and which itself is very variegated (Boyd 1988).

### 5.1.1 An Overview of Catalonia

Catalonia is at present governed under the statute of autonomy of 1979, derived from the Spanish constitution of 1978. The supreme body of government in the region is the "Generalitat," a body of ancient origin and history headed by a president, who is elected by the Catalan parliament[67].

Catalonia has for centuries been proud of its early democratic institutions, which differed from those of the rest of Spain. There were early parliaments or 'cortes' in Castille and Leon, but their only function was to raise taxes for the monarch. The Catalan corts also functioned as tax-raising bodies, but they developed a much stronger role in relation to the crown. For instance, by not allowing the class structure to broaden, but instead to narrow (the opposite took place in Castile and Leon).

Forty years of Franco's dictatorship brought cultural as well as political repression. However, Catalan culture life survived and reemerged, along with a widespread sentiment for the autonomy of Catalonia. Shortly after Franco's death in 1975, the so called "Generalitat"[68] was reestablished and has been the Catalan establishment pressuring the central government on the fulfillment of all its conditions down to the last letter.

Furthermore, the Spanish socialist government was and still is in need of Catalan support, headed by the president of the Generalitat, to remain in power after the last general elections in 1993[69]. Thus, the Catalans do play a very important role in Spanish politics at the present moment.

The Catalan people do not see themselves simply as a regional body. They are the representatives of a nation which may not have the status of a nation-state but does have all the other attributes of nationhood: language, literature, historical boundaries, and a small viable economy[70].

There are Catalan idealists who are prepared to accept the challenges of European competition within the European markets because they see the European Union as the framework within which the nation-state as it is known will eventually fade away to be replaced by a federal Europe in which Catalonia will enjoy equal status and the same full nationhood as Belgium, the Netherlands, Denmark, and other small open European economies.

### 5.1.2 The Viability of Globalization and Economic Growth of Catalonia when Integrated in to the EU[71]

#### *5.1.2.1 Catalonia: A European Federation*

Catalonia is, after Andalusia, the second largest autonomous community in number of citizens inside the nation-state of Spain. The region is located in the northeast corner of the Iberian Peninsula bordering the South of France and the Mediterranean Sea. It has a surface area of 31,930 sq. kilometers (12,772 sq. miles), and a population of approximately six million.

Because of its excellent geographical situation, Catalonia serves as a link between the center of Europe and the nations of the Mediterranean basin. This role as a crossroads of different cultures and influences has conditioned the historical and cultural evolution of Catalonia from its beginnings and has furthered the *commercial* character of its economy.

Its six million people represent about 16% of the Spanish population and the region occupies the ninth position in number of inhabitants in the group of 168 regions that comprise the European Union. With a population density of 191 hab/sq. km., it is above the European average of 144 hab/sq. km., but lower than Lombardy or Baden-Wuttemburg.

Because of its dynamic economy, it has traditionally been a receptor of important immigration movements from the rural areas of the rest of Spain, in particular Andalusia. Nevertheless, this process slowed down dramatically at the beginning of the eighties due to the impact of the global economic slow down and particularly of the Spanish economic crisis.

Because of the delay in the demographic transition, compared with other European developed regions, the proportion of young population is significantly higher. This has caused the labor supply to increase in recent years at a rate of 1.7%, constituting one of the most dynamic factors in Catalan economics.

Catalan is the official language of Catalonia, and it is understood by the majority of citizens, although about 30% of the population was born outside the region. Moreover, everyone speaks Spanish. The result of this bilinguism is that Catalans are predisposed to speaking other languages, which facilitates the globalization efforts of Catalonia.

Despite the progress in the tertiary sector, Catalonia is a strongly industrialized region in the European context with employment distributed as follows: agriculture 4.7%, industry 44.2%, and services 51.1%. Catalonia ranks very high as an industrilalized region within Europe. Of the four regions of Europe with the highest ratios of industrial employment to total employment, Catalonia ranks second only to the Baden-Wuttemburg region of Germany. Catalonia's 44.2% industrial employment ratio is only slightly less than Baden-Wuttemburg's 47%, a bit higher than Lombardy's 43.4%, and much higher than Rhone-Alpes' 34.7%.

### *5.1.2.2 Catalonia: A Small Viable Open Economy*

As examined in previous sections, the definition of small size is of course an arbitrary concept. The notion of smallness as used in conventional international economics is defined in terms of the neoclassical model of perfect competition which serves to facilitate a logical analysis of equilibrium forces that cannot help but reflect the real world situation.

But it can be observed within the European Union that there are small economies such as Denmark, Belgium, and Catalonia as well as large ones such as France, Germany, and Spain and intuitively notice that the size of nations *does matter*. A nation is confined to a small economic space such that it must use its size characteristics strategically in taking advantage of its linkages with the outside world.

Catalonia is in a unique and privileged position in taking advantage of its linkages with the outside world, since it already strategically uses its ties with the European Union members and with Central and South American nations. Catalan corporations possess strong trading ties with Germany, France, and Italy. Moreover, they are presented with many opportunities in world markets, something that has become easier in recent times with the rapid economic transition of Eastern European nations and the even faster economic re-structuring of Central and South American economies.

Based on the definition of smallness used in this study, Catalonia is a small open economy.

**Table 5–1. Classification of Catalonia's Economy**

| Catalonia | Data | Points |
|---|---|---|
| Population | | |
| (millions) | 6.1 | (3) |
| Size | | |
| (sq. Km.) | 31,930 | (4) |
| Export value | | |
| ($ millions) | 709.5 | (5) |
| Total Points | | (12) |

Based on the previous classification of nations within the European Union, Catalonia (12) would be the second smallest economy, Luxembourg (15) the smallest, and Austria (10), and Ireland (10) somewhat larger than the Catalan economy.

Senjur (1992, p.17) writes: "As small enterprises are economically viable by being competitive in some fields and being complementary to larger firms in other fields, so are small countries competitive and complementary to larger countries in the world market." Thus, the new wave of increased importance given to small enterprises in economic development and domestic competitiveness gives new support to the economic viability of small economies.

Hence, Catalonia should become more competitive and complementary to larger European members like France and Germany as the European federalism movement continues well into the XXI century.

#### *5.1.2.3 A View of Catalonia's Productive Structure*

As of 1985, Catalonia entered a period of strong expansion with an annual average growth rate close to 5%, greater than the Spanish rate of 3.7% and almost double of the European rate of 2.5%[72]. This growth rate rested on its favorable international and globalization context, and on its partial institutional flexibility through the modernization and restructuring of the productive systems in order to adapt to the new challenges and competition of the European unification process. This intense stage of growth has brought the Catalan GDP per capita, in 1991, to more than $17,000; 2% higher than the Spanish average.

The distribution of the Catalan GDP by sectors in 1991 was: primary (agriculture), 1.8%; construction 6.7%; industry 30.2%; and services 61.3%.

1. *Agricultural sector*. The Catalan agricultural structure is characterized by small size farms with a high level of mechanization. It produces sweet fruit totalling 40% of the Spanish annual production, most of the harvest is sold in the Spanish market. Olive oil is a product that has been developing larger export markets, worth more than $150 million in 1990, with the main clients being European Union members. The region also produces 40% of the poultry and pork in Spain.

Wine production is a growing sector that exported almost $150 million in 1990, with a wide presence in European and American markets. Another important agricultural food activity is the meat derivatives industry totalling around 35% of the Spanish production. Finally, Catalonia is, after Portugal, the second largest producer of cork and first in quality with an approximate production of more than $125 million, of which more than 50% is exported.

2. *Construction sector*. The construction sector, with an average annual growth rate of 9% in the last five years, has been one of the main driving forces of the Catalan economy in recent periods. Added to the recovery of private construction after 1988, increased demand for public works resulting from the selection of Barcelona as the site for the Summer Olympic Games of 1992 brought the production volume of the sector to around $10 billion in 1991.

3. *Industrial sector*. Catalonia leads the nation in this sector with 25% of Spanish industrial production. The most representative sectors

are metal, chemical, textile and food, machinery and equipment, and electronic materials. In recent years, the industrial structure of the region has progressively shifted from heavy basic industry to higher value added industry such as chemical-pharmaceutical, and higher-technology.

The business structure has been characterized by the predominance of small businesses oriented toward the Catalan and Spanish markets. However, in the last few years it has changed to the increasing internationalization of the Catalan economy, as evidenced by in the arrival of a new wave of FDI and multinational corporations[73]. At the same time, Catalan corporations are increasingly adopting strategies aimed at competing internationally.

4. *Service sector.* Services play an important role in the structure of the Catalan economy. The financial sector, transportation, and businesses services are complementary activities to the industrial development of the area, while health, education, and cultural services affect the welfare of the total population. Moreover, there is a very vibrant tourist sector[74], employing around 350,000 people and constituting the most important exporting sector of the territory.

#### *5.1.2.4 Specific Approaches of Catalan Globalization to Overcome Smallness and Secure Economic Growth*

How then can the contrast between empirical evidence and theoretical non-viability of small economies by explained? Small nations have disadvantages as examined earlier, but not necessary in all things. The major disadvantages can be eliminated by international trade and economic integration. Globalization is an essential precondition for the economic growth of any small economy.

The preceding analysis of the real world shows that compared to their larger counterparts, small nations are more "globalized" in terms of exploiting their opportunities in the global economy. The Catalan experience will now be analyzed.

1. *Trade focus.* Trade has long been an engine of growth and Catalonia is no exception. The commercial relations of Catalonia with ve increased dramatically since Spain entered the ity at the time in 1986. Thus, it is to no surprise that ny experienced an annual growth rate of almost 5% s (1986 to 1990).

Since then, exports and imports have increased at an annual double digit rate. The ratio of exports plus imports to GDP has increased from 36.2% in 1986 to 45.4% in 1991[75]. Much of this higher level of trade has been with other European Union members, in particular with France[76].

This observation jibes with Krugman's new emphasis on the geographical factors in economics. As he says: "We normally model countries as dimensionless points . . . and even trade among countries is usually given a sort of spaceless representation in which transport costs are zero for all goods that can be traded" (Krugman 1991, p. 2). If one were to theorize why Catalonia's largest trade partner is France, the conclusion would probably be that its transportation costs are minimum compared to transportation costs to other European nations; therefore, it is cheaper and more efficient. Hence, Krugman's view that nations are not distanceless points and that geographical factors directly *do* affect their trade relations seems right on the mark for the case of Catalonia and France.

Also, it is important to note that 71% of Catalan exports and 63% of its imports were within the European Union geographical zone in 1991. This lends further support to Krugman's point of proximity as an explanation of why Catalonia trades more with European nations (80.5% of total exports) than with the rest of the world (19.5% of total exports). Certainly the elimination of tariffs within the EU must play an important role as well.

2. *Specialization in "niche-market" goods*. The firms in small open economies, being confronted with the small size of the domestic market, must pursue diversification in both markets and products. Catalan corporations are already pursuing market diversification by trading with many countries such as France, Germany, Italy, Benelux, Portugal, United Kingdom, other Western and Eastern European nations, United States, Central and South America, and Japan. Furthermore, Catalan firms are undergoing a major re-structuring of their industrial production systems in order to pursue product diversification focusing on "niche-market" goods in the world market.

Indeed, this market and product differentiation is a complementary relationship that jibes once again with the imperfect competition theory of trade (Krugman 1990). Catalonia's exports are mainly metallurgical, chemical, vehicles, and textiles. Thus they are not *yet* extremely differentiated products that appeal to consumers worldwide. As a result.

Catalan exports are not specialized enough to reach specific "niche market" goods yet.

3. *Involvement in direct overseas businesses*. Here the focus will be on FDI alone. Small open economies which stress trade as an engine of growth—such as Catalonia—are likely to get involved in direct business operations abroad much earlier in their development path and to a much greater extent than their larger counterparts.

The presence of multinationals has been a regular phenomenon in the Catalan economy throughout the twentieth century. But in recent years since the opening up of the Catalan economy, inward FDI has increased ten fold from $1 billion in 1986 (1.2% of GDP) to $10 billion in 1991 (almost 9% of GDP)[77]. During the 1988–91 period, two thirds of FDI came from European Union members, in particular from France and Germany[78].

At the same time, there is an opening process of Catalan companies abroad in search of market diversification and lower production cost, but not yet in search of product diversification through "niche-market" goods. For example, companies with a competitive advantage in marketing are becoming multinationals, especially in the food sector. Moreover, firms which have fairly standardized production processes have also become multinationals in search of lower labor costs in North African countries, in particular those in the textile sector.

Undoubtedly, Catalonia is a clear example of a small economy's higher propensity to engage in direct overseas businesses, thus climbing its "development path" function of net outward investment as introduced by Dunning (1981).

In conclusion, inward FDI in Catalonia has facilitated its structural upgrading and supported the strong economic growth performance of the late 1980's and early 1990's. The hypothesis here is that Catalonia's small open economy, which has been proportionally more dependent on inward investment in its early stages of development, is becoming more oriented to outward investment as Catalan multinationals move their production facilities to North African countries and as the region advances in its economic development and becomes one of the most industrialized and sophisticated economies in Southern Europe.

4. *International economic integration*. One may ask whether the drawbacks of smallness can be overcome by economic integration. The European Union is perhaps the most successful attempt at economic integration in recent times. Catalonia, through Spain's integration in

1986, has already benefitted from the tremendous advantages of a larger European market.

The already advanced Catalan economy has not suffered to a large extent from the increased competition from neighboring larger European nations. Actually it has followed the development pattern of the stronger members of the EU, which has caused positive spillovers affecting both the amount and the quality of the factors of production due to technological advances and innovation (Krugman 1990). Thus, the EU has assisted in the differentiation of its manufactured products and facilitated the penetration of European "niche-market" goods by Catalan corporations.

### 5.1.3 Catalonia's Government

International competitiveness to some degree is a matter of institutions and institutional flexibility (as examined in Chapter Three). It is known that competitiveness requires flexibility, and that the flexibility of the Catalan economy depends on the complementary relationship between the public and the private sector. Institutional flexibility and change are imperative for the securing of competitiveness within the Catalan economy.

#### *5.1.3.1 Characteristics of Catalonia's Institutional System*

Catalonia, although an autonomous community within Spain, has its own parliament and government with the power to legislate and act on different matters, according with the Spanish constitution and the Statute of Autonomy of Catalonia. The several Catalan institutions of self-government form the so called "Generalitat."

The main characteristic of the Catalan institutional system is its *transperancy* and *stability*. The four elections since 1980 have been characterized by the victory of the nationalistic coalition, CiU (Convergence and Union), and its president Jordi Pujol. The coalition obtained the majority for the third consecutive time in the elections of 1992. Thus, the "rules of the game" are well known to the agents of the Catalan economy. Moreover, the "Generalitat" has a clear idea of what economic policy tools are accepted by the citizens and a total absence of political scandals.

The Catalan government has been very stable for the past fourteen years, but it is also surrounded by four factors that facilitate institutional change. First, Catalonia has an even more homogeneous cultural

Since then, exports and imports have increased at an annual double digit rate. The ratio of exports plus imports to GDP has increased from 36.2% in 1986 to 45.4% in 1991[75]. Much of this higher level of trade has been with other European Union members, in particular with France[76].

This observation jibes with Krugman's new emphasis on the geographical factors in economics. As he says: "We normally model countries as dimensionless points . . . and even trade among countries is usually given a sort of spaceless representation in which transport costs are zero for all goods that can be traded" (Krugman 1991, p. 2). If one were to theorize why Catalonia's largest trade partner is France, the conclusion would probably be that its transportation costs are minimum compared to transportation costs to other European nations; therefore, it is cheaper and more efficient. Hence, Krugman's view that nations are not distanceless points and that geographical factors directly *do* affect their trade relations seems right on the mark for the case of Catalonia and France.

Also, it is important to note that 71% of Catalan exports and 63% of its imports were within the European Union geographical zone in 1991. This lends further support to Krugman's point of proximity as an explanation of why Catalonia trades more with European nations (80.5% of total exports) than with the rest of the world (19.5% of total exports). Certainly the elimination of tariffs within the EU must play an important role as well.

2. *Specialization in "niche-market" goods*. The firms in small open economies, being confronted with the small size of the domestic market, must pursue diversification in both markets and products. Catalan corporations are already pursuing market diversification by trading with many countries such as France, Germany, Italy, Benelux, Portugal, United Kingdom, other Western and Eastern European nations, United States, Central and South America, and Japan. Furthermore, Catalan firms are undergoing a major re-structuring of their industrial production systems in order to pursue product diversification focusing on "niche-market" goods in the world market.

Indeed, this market and product differentiation is a complementary relationship that jibes once again with the imperfect competition theory of trade (Krugman 1990). Catalonia's exports are mainly metallurgical, chemical, vehicles, and textiles. Thus they are not *yet* extremely differentiated products that appeal to consumers worldwide. As a result, are metal, chemical, textile and food, machinery and equipment, and electronic materials. In recent years, the industrial structure of the region has progressively shifted from heavy basic industry to higher value added industry such as chemical-pharmaceutical, and higher-technology.

The business structure has been characterized by the predominance of small businesses oriented toward the Catalan and Spanish markets. However, in the last few years it has changed to the increasing internationalization of the Catalan economy, as evidenced by in the arrival of a new wave of FDI and multinational corporations[73]. At the same time, Catalan corporations are increasingly adopting strategies aimed at competing internationally.

4. *Service sector.* Services play an important role in the structure of the Catalan economy. The financial sector, transportation, and businesses services are complementary activities to the industrial development of the area, while health, education, and cultural services affect the welfare of the total population. Moreover, there is a very vibrant tourist sector[74], employing around 350,000 people and constituting the most important exporting sector of the territory.

#### *5.1.2.4 Specific Approaches of Catalan Globalization to Overcome Smallness and Secure Economic Growth*

How then can the contrast between empirical evidence and theoretical non-viability of small economies by explained? Small nations have disadvantages as examined earlier, but not necessary in all things. The major disadvantages can be eliminated by international trade and economic integration. Globalization is an essential precondition for the economic growth of any small economy.

The preceding analysis of the real world shows that compared to their larger counterparts, small nations are more "globalized" in terms of exploiting their opportunities in the global economy. The Catalan experience will now be analyzed.

1. *Trade focus.* Trade has long been an engine of growth and Catalonia is no exception. The commercial relations of Catalonia with other countries have increased dramatically since Spain entered the European Community at the time in 1986. Thus, it is to no surprise that the Catalan economy experienced an annual growth rate of almost 5% in the next five years (1986 to 1990).

1986, has already benefitted from the tremendous advantages of a larger European market.

The already advanced Catalan economy has not suffered to a large extent from the increased competition from neighboring larger European nations. Actually it has followed the development pattern of the stronger members of the EU, which has caused positive spillovers affecting both the amount and the quality of the factors of production due to technological advances and innovation (Krugman 1990). Thus, the EU has assisted in the differentiation of its manufactured products and facilitated the penetration of European "niche-market" goods by Catalan corporations.

### 5.1.3 Catalonia's Government

International competitiveness to some degree is a matter of institutions and institutional flexibility (as examined in Chapter Three). It is known that competitiveness requires flexibility, and that the flexibility of the Catalan economy depends on the complementary relationship between the public and the private sector. Institutional flexibility and change are imperative for the securing of competitiveness within the Catalan economy.

#### *5.1.3.1 Characteristics of Catalonia's Institutional System*

Catalonia, although an autonomous community within Spain, has its own parliament and government with the power to legislate and act on different matters, according with the Spanish constitution and the Statute of Autonomy of Catalonia. The several Catalan institutions of self-government form the so called "Generalitat."

The main characteristic of the Catalan institutional system is its *transperancy* and *stability*. The four elections since 1980 have been characterized by the victory of the nationalistic coalition, CiU (Convergence and Union), and its president Jordi Pujol. The coalition obtained the majority for the third consecutive time in the elections of 1992. Thus, the "rules of the game" are well known to the agents of the Catalan economy. Moreover, the "Generalitat" has a clear idea of what economic policy tools are accepted by the citizens and a total absence of political scandals.

The Catalan government has been very stable for the past fourteen years, but it is also surrounded by four factors that facilitate institutional change. First, Catalonia has an even more homogeneous cultural

pattern than other small nations perhaps due to the persecution and repression that its citizens have endured throughout the centuries, particularly in the twentieth century[79]. Second, it has a simple language situation with Catalan being the official language of the region, which is understood by the majority of its citizens[80]. Third, it possesses one of the finest educational systems in Europe with more than 175,000 students registered at more than 120 different universities and technical schools; therefore, having a well educated population. And finally, it spends more than 50% of its annual budget in education, social welfare, health, and social security providing for those in basic need, thus assuring a more even income distribution. Furthermore, short geographical distances facilitate face-to-face contacts[81]. These factors help to solve conflicts and communication problems, thus encouraging consensus among all parties. This may imply that it is easier to achieve coherence and flexibility in the Catalan institutional system than the Spanish one. A 'Nordic economic model' where government strongly assists in creating and allocating economic resources through specific macro-organizational strategies is already in place in Catalonia.

#### *5.1.3.2 Specific Approaches of the Implementation of Strategic Policies by Catalonia's Government.*

The kind of macro-organizational policies that the "Generalitat" follows are complementary to the interest of firms and markets, instead of substitutable of market imperfections. Thus, the Catalan government does place greater emphasis on strategies to strengthen public and private ties. These ties likely attract new capital, labor, and entrepreneurship that create dynamic comparative advantages through the development of new products and technologies, which indirectly provide a new focus on the niche-market of Catalonia's new trade economic space.

1. *An efficient economic environment.* The "Generalitat" has an impeccable record in setting a business-like economic climate for the entire region. First, it has been the Catalan government's goal to set an honest and corruption-free environment for businesses to follow. The outcome of the 1992 elections, in which the president obtained a unanimous majority for the third consecutive time, indicates the successful political leadership that Catalonia has enjoyed for the last fourteen years. Hence, it has provided a clear and stable economic climate, in which corporations have thrived.

And most importantly, it has recognized the importance of investing in its people to help them achieve their full potential in order to continue Catalonia's economic prosperity into the twenty first century. Education alone absorbed almost 25% of its budget in 1992.

2. *Good infrastructure*. Infrastructure provides the basic facilities and raw materials with which corporations can become more globalized by gaining access to new markets, customers, and suppliers. The 1992 Olympic selection of Barcelona brought Catalonia's infrastructure up to European levels. At the same time, Catalonia's economic expansion has led its government to initiate a series of road construction projects which, in part, will be financed by the private sector. Practically the entire system of cities in Catalonia has a first-class road connection.

Catalonia has two international airports, one in Barcelona and the other in Girona. The Barcelona airport is considered one of the most modern in Europe. It connects directly with more than 80 cities in the world and has a capacity up to 16 million passengers per year. Moreover, there are 39 ports along the 515 kilometers of the Catalan coast, nine of which are for commercial traffic[82]. The port of Barcelona has become the first in container traffic in the Mediterranean, ahead of Marseille and Genoa.

The "Generalitat" is dedicated to continue infrastructure improvements with its latest projects such as the expansion of the port of Barcelona, the installation of new telecommunication services and above all, the high-speed train connection with Europe. Two things should be pointed out: first, good infrastructure provides an advantage for globalization and international business activities, but alone does not ensure economic success. But second, the Catalan government is in the right direction to establish a long-lasting complementary relationship with the private sector, which will help to ensure economic growth.

3. *Support and incentives for the science and technology sectors.* The new challenge for Catalonia is to create a strategic plan incorporating science, educational, and industrial policy (see Chapter Three for further detail).

As stated above, the "Generalitat" heavily supports education, training, and research. One of the characteristics of the Catalan university system is the continuous increase in emphasis on technical studies. As of 1992, there were almost 50,000 students studying engineering, computer science, and scientific-experimental careers. Furthermore, Catalonia has a large network of public and private centers, in addition to the great concentration of R&D of large corporations with nearly 7,500 researchers and collaborators[83].

4. *Sustain and promote company exports*. Developing the export sector is an inevitable priority for Catalonia to become more economically viable for independence. The Catalan government already supports the sector by helping firms find new markets and become more internationalized.

Catalonia has 13 Official Chambers of Commerce, Industry, and Navigation that technically advise industry and the tertiary sector promoting their internationalization. In addition, the Official Chamber of Commerce, Industry, and Navigation of Barcelona, more than 100 years old, plays an important role by providing educational activities, especially in the field of domestic and foreign commerce. It assists in the internationalization of businesses by promoting commercial activities, fomenting cooperation between Catalan and foreign companies, and encouraging the participation of Catalan firms in European programs.

Furthermore, a large number of foreign Chambers of Commerce and commercial offices are present in Barcelona. These offer business promotion, technical assistance, and legal and fiscal consultation services.

Finally, the new challenge for Catalan leaders is to create new economic conditions and to continue those stated above which will provide a strong framework for entrepreneurial ingenuity to succeed as a small open economy within the new boundaries of the European Union.

### 5.1.4 Catalonia and Its Future

Catalonia, as an autonomous community of Spain, is and will continue being a key player in the new dynamic axis of the European economy. The center of European economic activity has traditionally been the Paris-London-Amsterdam triangle, with an extension to the South forming the so-called Central European Arc. Recently, this axis has been complemented with the emergence of a second arc, the so-called Mediterranean Arc. This second arc, with an area of 300,000 sq. kilometers and nearly 50 million people, is likely to become one of the main growth axes of the new European Union.

Economic activity in this area is based on the dissemination and utilization of new technologies (emphasized by the New Growth

Theory) and their application in consolidated industrial structures within the context of flexible manufacturing and/or flexible specialization production processes.

Catalonia is and will be an important and influential piece in this Mediterranean axis. The Catalan territory has a viable and vibrant small open economy based on five pillars: first, its geographical position and easy communications with the rest of the Mediterranean cities and Central Europe. Second, its broad and varied use of new technologies in the industrial sector propelling the region to become one of the leaders of economic growth among European regions. Third, its unexploited wealth of natural and physical resources. Fourth, its growing cities with important universities, active research laboratories, significant progress in new technologies, and vibrant cultural activity. And finally, its capital, Barcelona, still savoring the celebration of the 1992 Olympic Games and attracting economic activities and leading multinationals and institutions[84].

Nationalism, ethnic conflicts, repression, bitterness, history, and loyalties, not economic analysis, are probably some of the reasons why Catalonia wants more autonomy from the Spanish central government. But as Becker (1990, p. 20) says: "Whatever the motives, the statistics on actual performance show that dire warnings about the economic price suffered by small nations are not all warranted"; or as Becker (1994, p. 20) suggests: "Why so many mice are roaring. . . . Smallness can be an asset in the division of labor in the modern world, where economies are linked through international transactions. Nationalism is merely riding the crest of world trade to forge new nations."

Certainly, Catalonia is *no exception*, and it can easily be the next Estonia[85], Latvia, or Lithuania with or without Spain's political authority and economic leadership.

## 5.2 NEW ZEALAND: A COUNTRY CASE STUDY

New Zealand serves as a good case study for other nations to examine the processes of structural and economic adjustment. The country's economic structure has strong similarities with both developed and less-developed nations. It is a small open economy with a large agricultural export sector, but with a high income level. New Zealand has followed a more import-substitution and generally interventionist economic strategy than other high-income nations. Moreover, New Zealand is an island state with high transportation costs.

Because of the country's size, isolation, cultural heritage, and historical ties, New Zealanders and its Kiwi character of individualism combined with entrepreneurial spirit, have encouraged and supported a specific form of economic and political organization over long periods of time.

New Zealand was a leader in the development of the so-called "Welfare State" during the 1930's and universal accident compensation in the 1970's. Nationalization and state control of industry were important throughout most of the British settlement. Moreover, the New Zealand government tended to rely heavily on economic regulations, trade policy instruments, subsidies and protection of industries at all levels. In short, government planning and intervention have played a major role in New Zealand's development until 1982 (Lattimore 1987, p. 34 & 35).

More recently, New Zealand found itself on the verge of economic disaster. The crisis was prompted by massive overseas borrowing, increasing failures of national state enterprises, and loose monetary policy which created an inflationary surge which hit a peak of 17% in 1982. New Zealand's government opted for a radical change in economic policy toward a more open and free market system in 1984. In just ten years, New Zealand has become one of the most vibrant economies in the world with a modern and competitive economy.

### 5.2.1 The Emergence of New Zealand

New Zealand was first discovered by Abel Tasman of the Dutch East India Corporation, 150 years after the discovery of America, in 1642. But, it was not until 1769 that Captain Cook circumnavigated and mapped the two main islands, North and South Islands. New Zealand soon after emerged as a major trading region with exports of bizarre and exotic commodities, and very close ties with Great Britain. The "Treaty of Waitangi" is regarded as the founding document of New Zealand. First signed at Waitangi in 1840, the Treaty was an agreement between the Maori people and the British Crown, in which the Maori people ceded sovereignty over New Zealand to the British Queen, who in return affirmed for the Maori their status as the indigenous people of New Zealand (Laking 1963, p. 5–24).

New Zealand, despite its short history, offers a remarkable record of support for the principles of democracy inherited from the British tradition. Furthermore, this nation is not in the economic sense a fully developed country, but in the 155 years which have passed since the first organized settlement from Great Britain, New Zealand is one of the world's largest exporters of primary commodities. At the same time, it has attained a standard of living measured in GNP per capita of $12,300, which is much higher than some European countries such as Greece and Portugal, similar to others such as Ireland and Spain, and not too far behind Great Britain (World Tables 1994).

The economic success that this small open economy is experiencing in the mid 1990's (with a GDP growth rate of 5.3% in 1994 and a forecasted GDP growth rate of 4.5% in 1995[86]) can be attributed to two factors. The first is the realization of the necessity of further outward orientation and the importance of FDI in economic growth during the late 1960's; thus, becoming less dependent on Great Britain, its main trading partner at the time. The second is the massive structural reform of the economy's productive capacity through decreasing government influence over the management of the economy starting in 1984, as well as a continuous understanding of the importance of exports and FDI as the main engines of economic growth.

### 5.2.2 The Viability of Globalization and Economic Growth of New Zealand

#### *5.2.2.1 The Problem*

In the early 1970's, New Zealand was faced with chronic labor shortages and a huge welfare system as a result of which there were plenty of jobs for low-skilled labor with low wages in heavily protected industries, thus producing overpriced goods for consumers with very little to no choices. This arrangement was supported by more or less guaranteed access for its products to the British markets. Moreover, New Zealanders seemed complacent with their colonial British dependence and abysmal levels of productivity growth.

The turning point for the New Zealand economy came in 1973 with the first oil shock and the entrance of Great Britain into the EEC. New Zealand's economic environment was suddenly rocked by external economic conditions.

New Zealand tried to ignore the harsh economic realities at the time. The government engaged in heavy borrowing overseas, industry support through subsidies (including the agricultural sector which was already competitive internationally), careless macro-economic policies leading to double digit inflation (which became the norm instead of the exception), and finally, funding huge energy projects, which became total failures costing the taxpayers billions of dollars (Lattimore 1987).

Summers and Heston's (1988) data shows that the performance of the New Zealand economy compared with its neighbor Australia had worsened, particularly in the decade of the 1970's. New Zealand's GDP growth rates went from 3.8% for the 1960–1973 period, to .3% for the 1973–1980 period, to 1.8% for the 1980–1988 period. In contrast, Australia's GDP growth rates went from 5.2%, to 2.7%, to 3.1% respectively for the same periods; indeed, reflecting a wider gap of 2.4% in the 1973–1980 period, compared to the 1.4% gap in the other two periods. Most alarming was the increasing gap of its growth rates compared to the newly industrializing economies of South East Asia.

The underlying causes of New Zealand's economic troubles were partly structural in nature. Government intervention to compensate for market imperfections for the most part prevented corporations from making the necessary structural adjustments to accommodate the changing global economic environment.

Moreover, Akoorie (1994) points out a New Zealand economic survey prepared by OECD in 1980. The survey highlighted problems such as the agricultural sector was becoming even more vulnerable to outside shocks, the high cost structure in the manufacturing sector was causing it to lose competitiveness internationally, and the exchange rate was becoming extremely overvalued and was generating upward pressure on export prices, thus reducing the competitiveness of the exporting industries.

Finally, in 1982 when inflation hit a peak of almost 20%, government reacted by freezing all prices and wages. Over the next two years, the distortions became even larger, and New Zealand suffered a currency crisis (Myers 1992, p. 20).

Countries have frequently changed course during an economic crisis. New Zealand was no exception, but it surely was slow in reacting, almost to the point where economic disaster became imminent. It will be shown later how in only eight years, New Zealand has been able to turn its economy around and enjoy a high rate of economic growth in 1994 with a modern, competitive economy, and a new look and attitude toward businesses and the outside world.

### 5.2.2.2 New Zealand: A Small Open Economy

New Zealand is located in the South Pacific Ocean, 6,500 kilometers south-west of Hawai and 1,900 kilometers east of Australia, with a land area of 268,676 square kilometers compromised of two main islands, the North and the South Island, and a number of small adjacent islands.

About 134,000 square kilometers of New Zealand's land area is pasture and arable land. The terrain is mostly mountainous and hilly with many lakes and rivers providing valuable sources of hydro-electric power.

The population is about 3.4 million with more than 50% living in the five urban areas of Wellington, the capital, Auckland, Christchurch, Hamilton, and Dunedin. The population is mainly European of British descendants (79%), with New Zealand Maori (13%), Pacific Islanders (5%), and other ethnic groups (3%). It also has a high degree of social and political stability and a modern social welfare system, with a high rate of intermarriage among these groups[87].

As stated previously, the definition of a small economy is an arbitrary concept, but it can be observed within Oceania a large economy like Australia and a small economy like New Zealand, and intuitively notice that the size of nations again *does matter.* A nation is confined to a small economic space such that it must use its linkages with the outside world.

New Zealand has been taking advantage of its linkages with the outside world since its origins by becoming a major exporter of agricultural and natural resources in its early development. Furthermore, New Zealanders did dramatically increase their linkages with the outside world since the 1984 radical change of economic policy. They are presented with many new opportunities in world markets, something that has become easier in recent times with the so-called "East Asian Miracle," (the rapid growth of the newly industrializing countries of East Asia).

Based on the definition of smallness used in this study, New Zealand is a small open economy, as shown in Table 5–2.

**Table 5–2. Classification of New Zealand's Economy**

| New Zealand | Data | Points |
|---|---|---|
| Population (millions) | 3.4 | (4) |

| | | |
|---|---|---|
| Size (sq. Km.) | 268,676 | (0) |
| Export Value ($ millions) | 6,859.8 | (3) |
| Total Points | | (7) |

*5.2.2.3 A View of New Zealand's Productive Structure*[88]

As of 1984, New Zealand entered a new period of structural economic reform. In less than a decade, New Zealand is beginning to reap the benefits of its extensive reform process. The economy grew by 2.9% in 1992–1993 and 5.3% in 1994. Inflation has remained below 2% since 1991. In addition, the 1993–1994 budget was in surplus by .6% of GDP.

This economic performance rests on its government liberalization process, its institutional flexibility, and its favorable international and globalization context, particularly as shown by an expansion in export earnings in non-commodity manufactures. This intense economic transition has brought the New Zealand GDP per capita in 1992 to more than $12,000, narrowing the gap with Australia's 1992 GDP per capita of $17,260 (World Tables 1994).

New Zealand has a mixed economy which operates on free market principles. It has sizeable manufacturing and service sectors complementing a highly efficient agricultural sector. The economy is strongly trade oriented, with exports of goods and services totalling 31% of GDP in 1993. The distribution of the New Zealand GDP by sectors in 1993 was as follows: primary 11.5%, manufacturing 17.4%, services 55.3%, and government 15.8%. Each sector will now be examined in more detail.

1. *Primary sector*. Agriculture employed almost 10% of the labor force in 1993 and contributed 6% to GDP. These products generated $9.1 billion in exports, amounting to 49% of the country's total exports for 1993. Significant export crops include nashi, kiwi, berryfruit, honey, flowers, onions, squash, and wine. Moreover, livestock was very significant with 62.5 million animals commercially farmed.

Forestry and logging, manufacture of wood products, and manufacture of paper products accounted for 5.7% of GDP in 1991. Forestry supports an important export industry with more than 65% of wood being exported. The value of forestry products was $2,278 million or 12.5% of New Zealand's total merchandise exports. The largest markets for forestry exports are Australia, Japan, South Korea, and Taiwan. Fishing has developed into a major New Zealand export industry as well, accounting for 6% of total merchandise exports. More than 80% of production is exported mainly to United States, Japan, and Australia.

Finally, New Zealand has significant natural energy resources such as coal, natural gas, oil, iron sand, gold, sand, gravel, and electricity. Since 1984, the government has been engaged in the removal of franchises and the deregulation of the previously controlled oil, gas, and electricity markets in order to provide a more competitive market structure.

2. *Manufacturing sector.* The proportion of the labor force employed in this sector was 16.8% in 1993 and it contributed 17.4 to GDP in 1991. As in the rest of the economy, major structural changes have developed in this sector since 1984. Tariffs have been systematically reduced, except in motor vehicles, footwear, clothing, and textiles.

Manufacturing output increased by 16.3% between 1991 and 1993, fueled by an increase in exports due to the improved competitiveness of the nation. The biggest manufacturing sectors are food processing, motor vehicle assembly, electronics, chemicals, and paper and printing.

3. *Service sector.* The continued development of the New Zealand economy has caused a steady growth in service industries. This sector accounted for almost 75% of GDP in 1991 and employed 72.4% of the labor force in 1993.

In 1984, the financial markets were liberalized, and most direct controls on the financial services were lifted with impressive results such as rapid growth in money market activity, development of a secondary market in government securities, introduction of forward contracts, options, and exchange rate futures, and instruments to hedge interest and exchange rate risk.

Moreover, New Zealand has a significant infrastructure of small businesses serving the larger economy such as real state agents, advertising and public relations agencies, insurance brokers, and financial, accounting, and legal professionals.

Also, the transportation sector is vital to New Zealand's economic activity. The country's transport system has had to adjust not only to New Zealand's dependence on international trade and its remoteness from many of its trading partners, but also to its rugged terrain, scattered population, and the division of the country into two main islands. The efficiency of the transportation infrastructure, including networks of roads and railways linked to ports and airports, has played a major role in New Zealand's economic recovery.

Another prominent sector within the service industry is tourism. It is the largest single source of foreign exchange, with preserved natural resources, unspoiled scenery, and a range of outdoor activities making New Zealand a paradise for the vigorous tourist. During 1993, 1.1 million visitors entered New Zealand providing $3.23 billion in foreign exchange. As of 1992, tourism accounted for 5.3% of GDP and employed 6.5% of the total labor force.

Furthermore, New Zealand has the most sophisticated telecommunication sector in the world and was ranked number one by the "World Competitiveness Report, 1993." This sector has experienced dramatic changes recently since its extensive deregulation, with the customer premises equipment market being systematically opened to competition since 1987.

4. *Government sector.* Again since 1984, government has been reappraising the State's role in commercial activities, with the objectives of lowering the exposure of the state to uncertainty and business risk and improving productivity.

Since 1987, twenty five state-owned enterprises were privatized. Additionally, government has introduced business incentives to its production of goods and services in order to improve efficiency. The government is involved in finance and insurance, housing, airway and railway transportation, communications, coal and electricity production, and management of natural resources.

#### *5.2.2.4 Specific Strategies of New Zealand's Globalization to Overcome Smallness and to Secure Economic Growth*

Small economies have disadvantages as examined previously but not necessary in all sectors of their productive capacity. Most of these disadvantages can be eliminated through international trade and economic integration. Globalization is an essential precondition for the economic growth of any small state, and New Zealand is no exception.

The preceding analysis of the real world showed that compared to their larger counterparts, small economies are more "globalized" in terms of exploiting their opportunities in world markets. New Zealand's experience will now be explored.

1. *Trade focus.* Trade has long been known as an engine of growth for New Zealand, especially in its early development thanks to primary exports such as agriculture and forestry. Moreover, its economic recovery is continuing to reinforce export growth as a primary positive contributor to economic performance. In 1992, the ratio of exports plus imports to GNP was almost 45% greater than its larger counterpart of Australia with a ratio of 26% (World Tables 1994).

Since the major economic and structural reforms of 1984 in favor of economic liberalization, exports and imports have increased by 60.5% from 1984 to 1992. Much of this growth in trade has been with Australia, due to their comprehensive agreements on closer economic relations[89] (World Tables 1994).

New Zealand has focused increasingly on developing new linkages with other trading partners and has also diversified its export markets over recent decades[90]. In 1950, Great Britain accounted for almost 67% of New Zealand's exports; as of 1993 it accounted for only 6.5%. New Zealand's main trading regions in the world in 1993 were Australia 19.3%, Japan 15.3%, Europe 13.5%, United States 12.2%, East Asia 15.3%, other 24.4%[91] (New Zealand: Economic and Financial Overview 1994).

Once again, this observation jibes with Krugman's new emphasis on the geographical factors in economics (1991). If one were theorize why New Zealand's largest trade partner is Australia, a reasonable conclusion would be that its transportation costs are not as high as transportation costs to Great Britain (once its main trading partner); thus, it is cheaper and more efficient to trade with Australia than with any other country. Hence, Krugman's view that for some purposes it is helpful to ignore the fact that countries are distanceless points and that geographical factors *do* affect their trade relations, as in the case of New Zealand with Australia is supported.

In addition, it is important to note that almost 50% of New Zealand's exports and 47% of its imports were with East Asian economies in 1993. (New Zealand: Economic and Financial Overview 1994). This lends further support to Krugman's point of the importance of proximity.

2. *Specialization in "niche-market goods.* The companies in small open economies, being confronted with the small size of the domestic market, have to pursue diversification in both markets and products. New Zealand's businesses are already pursuing market diversification by trading with as many as twenty different countries located all over

the world. Moreover, the New Zealand economy and its corporations too are undergoing a major re-structuring of their industrial production systems jointly with national goods, labor, and capital markets, and government management in order to pursue product diversification focusing on "niche-market" goods in global markets.

Indeed, this market and product differentiation is a complementary relationship that jibes with the imperfect competition theory of trade (Krugman 1990). New Zealand's exports are mainly agricultural products such as meat, wool, and dairy, which are processed and packaged as consumer products. Also, horticulture products such as fish, fruit, timber, and pulp and paper products are becoming significant export commodities.

Moreover, exports of non-food products such as plastic, textiles, aluminum frames, electric fencing, furniture, electronics, telecommunications, and computer software have expanded rapidly over the last decade. These exports have opened new and promising markets for New Zealand's firms. But these goods perhaps with the exception of electronics, telecommunications, and computer software, are not *yet* extremely differentiated products that appeal to consumers worldwide. As a result, New Zealand's exports are still in the early stages of specialization in order to reach specific "niche-market" goods.

Despite the lack of "niche-market" goods, there are some encouraging signs within the electronics and the software industry. For example, the value of New Zealand's exports of enhanced electronic products is between $200 and $300 million, serving developed nations such as United States, Japan, Germany, and Australia (Pyne 1992). The software industry is another example. According to the managing director of the Bank of New Zealand, Mr. Pyne:

> "We are only small players in the global market . . . but there are niches where we have excelled. . . . A diverse customer base has forced software developers to create products offering a wide range of functions than those available internationally." (The New Zealand Investment Conference, 1992)

Again, software products are exported to developed nations with 65% of these exports serving Australia, the United States, and Canada. Currently, there are more than 600 companies developing applications or systems software for perhaps only one client at a time (Tradenz Report 1993–1994).

3. *Involvement in direct overseas businesses.* The focus here will be on FDI alone. Small open economies such as New Zealand realize the importance of inward FDI as an engine of growth. Thus they become involved with direct international business operations much earlier in their development and to a much greater extent than their larger counterparts.

The presence of multinationals, especially from Britain, has been a regular phenomenon in New Zealand's economics since the discovery of the century. But in recent years, since the massive re-structuring of the economy, the wide fluctuation levels of investment reflect the high degree of uncertainty about the commitment of government within the international community to continue the structural reforms of the goods, labor, and capital markets, and the reform of the government and its monetary and fiscal economic policies.

During the 1987–1993 period, more than two thirds of inward FDI came from Australia, Britain, United States, and Canada, particularly from Australia. Singapore and Taiwan have also increased their FDI in New Zealand in that same period. Additionally, the further significance of FDI in this small open economy is exhibited by the ratio of FDI to GDP between 1990 and 1991 averaging 4% of GDP in New Zealand, compared with 1.9% of GDP in Australia (Akoorie 1994, p 27).

At the same time, there has been tremendous growth in outward FDI, especially to Australia and Britain, with an increase from $NZ 54 million in 1984 to $NZ 3,961 million in 1990. For example, companies with ownership specific advantages in the forestry, pulp, and paper sectors have expanded operations in Canada. Furthermore, firms with ownership specific advantages in engineering and software industries, acquired through the flexibility and small scale attention to specific problems, have entered the South East Asian markets (Akoorie 1994).

Undoubtedly, New Zealand is a clear example of a small economy's higher propensity to engage in direct overseas businesses suggesting a shift in the "development path" function of net outward investment introduced by Dunning (1981).

Finally, inward FDI in New Zealand, particularly from Great Britain, has facilitated its economic development since its settlement. More recently, it has also facilitated its massive economic reforms and has supported its economic recovery of the 1990's. New Zealand's small open economy, which has been proportionally more dependent on inward investment in its early stages of development, is becoming partially more oriented to outward investment as it continues its structural reforms and economic recovery and becomes one of the most vibrant economies in Oceania. As of 1990, inward FDI was $NZ 2,894 and outward FDI was $NZ 3,961 (Akoorie 1994)[92].

4. *Strategic management of exchange rates and price stability.* Exchange rates are the link between domestic and global prices. The more "globally oriented" a nation is, the more sensitively and strategically it manages and uses the exchange rate mechanism. In other words, the exchange rate is a key policy variable for a small open economy with New Zealand being no exception[93].

Exchange rate policy in both Australia and New Zealand in the 1970's and 1980's was characterized by radical modifications. During the 1970's and early 1980's, both countries operated pegged or managed exchange rates. New Zealand's exchange rate regime had gone from being fixed to sterling, to fixed to the U.S. dollar, to fixed against a trade-weighted basket, and then to a crawling peg against another weighted basket of currencies. However, New Zealand moved to a freely floating exchange rate in 1985, after a massive devaluation of 20% of its currency in 1984 and just one year after the launching of its massive structural reforms[94] (Sherwin 1990).

As examined previously New Zealand is mainly a small commodity-exporting country. Thus its exchange rate becomes even more vulnerable to external shocks and rising world commodity prices. For example, a strong demand from its main trading partners with rising world commodity prices puts upward pressure on New Zealand's exchange rate and export prices in order to ensure equilibrium in the goods market. But the non-commodity sectors are greatly affected by the rise of the exchange rate, thus losing competitiveness and market share (Blundell-Wignall and Gregory 1990).

Thus, New Zealand has even a greater need to strategically manage its exchange rate due to wild swings in world commodity prices which create short-run and perhaps long-run currency volatility under a floating regime. But simply a sterilized intervention, even though it may have little or no impact on fundamental exchange rate movements, can provide the market with more direction when market inefficiencies dominate[95].

Typically, small nations need larger real depreciations in order to weather the storms of tandem disturbances; therefore, small countries must adopt appropriate macroeconomic policies to keep the exchange rate somewhat undervalued, thus providing support for the exporting sector. The New Zealand experience during the 1987–88 terms-of-trade cycle, which seemed to have been less inflationary than previous external shocks, was absorbed rather well when the $NZ depreciated around 10% against the U.S. dollar in nominal terms and almost 17% in real terms from 1987 to 1989 (IMF, International Financial Statistics 1991–92).

Moreover, New Zealand under a true flexible exchange rate, has been very effective in attaining price stability through the effective use of monetary policy and the partially strategic management of exchange rates without choking off its economic recovery. Blundell-Wignall and Gregory (1990, p.268) write:

> "The choice of a broadly floating exchange rate is essential for low-inflation monetary policy in a commodity-exporting country . . . some form of exchange rate management is always likely to be necessary for effective monetary policy."

New Zealand's economic data speaks for itself. In 1986, annual inflation surpassed 15%. As of 1993, the annual inflation rate was 1.5%, one the lowest inflation rates among developed nations[96].

Additionally, it should be pointed out that price stability is not limited to the monetary authorities, but is also a part of a total macroeconomic approach that avoids excesses in wage policies, budget deficits, and protection of industries. Since the 1984 structural reforms, New Zealand has also enjoyed downward pressure on prices due to higher competition within the economy thanks to massive deregulation of markets and the privatization of state monopolies, international competition thanks to enormous trade liberalization efforts, and finally, a budget surplus of .6% of GDP[97]; thus, providing the proper economic environment for price stability.

5. *International economic integration.* Many economists ask the question "Can smallness be overcome by economic integration?" The EU may perhaps be the most successful attempt at economic integration in recent history, but other economic integration strategies such as ASEAN and APEC are flourishing around the globe.

Since the 1930's border protection has been very important to the New Zealand economy, thus allowing for the growth of a viable domestic industry. But instead, the main result was a reduction of goods available in the market place along with higher prices. The cost of this isolation became alarming by the early 1980's, and the first major change was the negotiation of the Australia New Zealand Closer

Economic Relations Treaty in 1983 (ANZCERT), with the provision to join the two countries in a free trade area by 1995.

New Zealand has undoubtedly benefited from new trade alliances with other nations around the world and particularly with its closest trading partners. It is also a member of APEC, (Asia Pacific Economic Cooperation) with the main objective of developing regional trade and economic integration among its members and has been a fervent supporter of the GATT agreement.

These trade linkages, along with the major structural reforms of trade liberalization, have affected both the amount and quality of its factors of production due to technological advances and innovation (Krugman 1990). This has assisted New Zealanders in the differentiation of manufactured products and the penetration of East Asian "niche-market" goods. New Zealand's exports of manufactures grew by almost 90% from 1983 to 1992 (World Tables 1994), which indeed has assisted New Zealand to become the ninth most competitive nation in the world (World Competitiveness Report 1994).

### 5.2.3 New Zealand's Government

International competitiveness to some degree is a matter of institutions and institutional flexibility (as discussed in Chapter Three). It is known that competitiveness requires flexibility, and the flexibility already exhibited by the New Zealand economy found its best ally in the new government elected in 1984.

#### *5.2.3.1 Characteristics of New Zealand's Institutional Structure*

New Zealand became a sovereign state with a democratic parliamentary government after the signing of the Treaty of Waitangi back in 1840, when the indigenous Maori people yielded sovereignty over New Zealand to the Queen of England. The New Zealand Constitution Act of 1852 provided for the establishment of a Parliament with an elected House of Representatives. Universal suffrage was introduced before the turn of the nineteenth century in 1893. Furthermore, the new Constitution Act of 1986 updated and provided for a legislative body, an executive and administrative structure and specific protection for the judiciary body[98]. (New Zealand: Economic and Financial Overview, 1994).

The main characteristic of New Zealand's institutional system is its *flexibility*. Since the 1984 structural reforms, the government has dramatically shifted gears from an interventionism and protectionism mode to one of liberalization. In the last decade, New Zealand has become one of the most open and free small economies in the world.

This major transformation has occurred thanks to several factors: first, years of procrastination leading to economic chaos providing a sense of urgency; second, a high degree of social and political stability rooted in British influence and tradition; third, the possession of skilled labor thanks to compulsory schooling years in the tertiary sector and the work place; fourth, a long established record of promoting a more even distribution of income through a generous welfare system accounting for almost 25% of GDP in 1993, and providing health, education, income support for low income families, and a range of other benefits and pensions; and finally, a clear and transparent economic plan put forward through a reformed government which was willing to undertake such imperative changes.

In addition, the fact that the peculiar geographical arrangement of the nation with many small islands adjacent to the main two islands does not facilitate face-to-face contacts, which thus creates a lack of communication and discourages consensus among all parties. This may provide some evidence of the slow response from both the public and the private sector to the economic difficulties that troubled New Zealand since the early 1970's.

#### *5.2.3.2 Specific approaches of New Zealand's Government Turnaround Policies*

The kind of economic policies that the New Zealand government has implemented in the last ten years have been complementary to the interests of private businesses and markets, instead of the previous substitutable strategies of market imperfections.

Hence, the new reformed government has placed greater emphasis on economic strategies to strengthen public and private ties. These new strategies have to a certain extent provided a more conducive environment in which to do business in the country. In fact, New Zealand is ranked number one in the category of describing the extent to which government policies are conducive to competitiveness (World Competitiveness Report 1994, p. 24).

Moreover, New Zealand's economic recovery, due in part to the government's structural reforms in goods, labor, and capital markets, has attracted foreign capital and entrepreneurship that have already and will continue to assist in the creation of dynamic comparative advantages through the development of innovative products and technologies, which indirectly provide a new focus on the niche-markets of New Zealand's trading economic space.

1. *An efficent economic environment.* The New Zealand government has introduced many reforms in the markets for goods, capital, and labor over the last decade.

In the goods market, policy reforms such as removal of border protection, removal of industry assistance, introduction of a uniform-rate of VAT, infrastructural reforms, and new competition policies have been implemented. These strategies are the main contributors of a goods market exhibiting greater efficiency, productivity, dynamism, and flexibility.

In the capital market, policy reforms such as removal of interest rate controls, removal of exchange rate controls, abolition of ratio requirements, independence of the Reserve Bank, new monetary policy with inflation control as the main objective, and formation of new banks increasing competition have vastly improved the economic environment. All these changes provide the small saver in New Zealand and large international investors with increased confidence in new investment opportunities, which in conjunction with greater competition has served to increase the level of efficiency in the allocation of financial capital.

In the labor market, policy reforms such as a flatter tax scale, tighter eligibility rules for welfare benefits, new apprenticeship and training programs, higher education affordability, and new industrial relations law dealing with voluntary unionism, enterprise bargaining, and fixed term contracts have contributed to a more efficient labor market. It is difficult to asses all the impacts of these new policies, but overall workers operate in a tougher environment with a much greater pace of change. In addition, there are more opportunities for training and advancement, which are available to all, not only the privileged. New Zealand has moved from a closely regulated labor market with centralized pay fixing and weak training processes to a new milieu with better opportunities to be productive, more chances to improve skills, more freedom to organize work arrangements, and a growing number of jobs.

It should be pointed out that the combination of these reform policies in the three markets of the economy are complementary of each other. For example, the results and performance in the goods market depend in part on the success of the capital and labor market.

Furthermore, reforms in government management such as corporatization and privatization of companies, restructuring of the accounting system, and public sector employment tied to performance have increased government's accountability and responsibility to its citizens (Prebble 1994).

Hence, New Zealand officials have put in place a more clear and stable economic climate in which corporations are willing to invest and are beginning to thrive.

2. *Good infrastructure*. Infrastructure provides the basic facilities and raw materials with which firms can become more globalized by gaining access to new markets, customers, and suppliers. New Zealand's isolation from the rest of the world makes the development of excellent infrastructure facilities in air transport, port access, and telecommunications absolutely imperative.

Indeed, the telecommunications industry is of great importance to the New Zealand economy, not only domestically linking the two main islands and the numerous small islands adjacent to them, but also internationally linking this small open economy to world events and information. The World Competitiveness Report ranked New Zealand number one in the telecommunications area in 1993, not surprising because of its necessity to rely on foreign markets for economic growth and to overcome small domestic markets.

New Zealand also has a railway system connecting all major population centers and including three island rail ferries. Around 90% of New Zealand's trade is carried by sea. Port reforms are being experienced by corporatization and privatization of many ports and by new technologies. And finally, the opening of New Zealand's air space to foreign competition in 1987 led to a major upgrading of its major airports. (New Zealand: Economic and Financial Overview 1994).

3. *Support and incentives for science and technology*. As stated above, New Zealand's government does support education, training, and technical careers, but R&D has taken a back position. New Zealand's real growth in total expenditure on R&D from 1983 to 1991 has been only .50%. In 1981 New Zealand spent about 1.4% of GDP on R&D; in 1991 it spent only .87% of GDP, less than any other developed nation except for Spain, Portugal, and Greece (World Competitiveness Report 1993).

The government's share of R&D amounts to about 60% with no dramatic decline over the last decade, but business R&D has declined and is significantly less than in other developed countries when measured as a share of GDP[99].

As of 1991, New Zealand only had 15,000 R&D scientists and engineers in industry. This is in sharp contrast with Sweden, for example, which had over 115,000 private sector R&D scientists and engineers. This underscores the need for further dissemination of science and technology throughout the country (World Competitiveness Report 1993).

But the government is starting to recognize the importance of innovation, science, and technology through private as well as public investments. In connection with the allocation of public funds in R&D, there have been substantial changes in recent years to the structures and processes for science awareness and delivery. These changes have included the creation of a small policy Ministry of Research, Science, and Technology, the creation of ten Crown Research Institutes to conduct R&D, and the continuation of a small Technology for Business Growth program for partnership projects with individual businesses (Tradenz 1993/94).

4. *Sustain and promote company exports.* Expanding and diversifying the export sector is an inevitable priority for New Zealand to maintain its economic recovery. The New Zealand Trade Development Board (TRADENZ) lead by the Minister of Trade Negotiations published a 1993/94 report entitled "Stretching for Growth: Building an Export Strategy for New Zealand," in which it outlines strategies to finding new markets and becoming more internationalized.

Taking a closer look at the report, it suggests three fronts where activity needs to progress simultaneously, namely business capability, infrastructure, and market development.

In business capability, TRADENZ promotes export industries by creating partnerships and alliances, working with businesses and professional societies to develop world marketing plans, providing information and new trends on overseas markets, contributing to high quality standards, and promoting the use of strategic planning in export development.

In infrastructure, TRADENZ recognizes that people are the most valuable resource of New Zealand thus promoting education, training, and academic excellence through different programs. It also provides guidance and support to R&D, investment funds, financial infrastructure, and environmental awareness.

In market development, TRADENZ with 43 offices overseas provides the following: first, it expands market access through negotiations of trade agreements with other nations. Second, it provides market knowledge and information on foreign markets such as market size, access requirements, regulatory conditions and environment, market structure, competitor's activities, technological developments, market trends, consumer research, and contacts. Third, it increases overseas market presence of New Zealand's export companies through promotional activities. And finally, it provides a branding strategic plan, especially for those exporters moving to differentiated products. For example, TRADENZ and the New Zealand Tourism Board have created a joint venture creating a platform for New Zealand exporters to use the country as an additional point of differentiation.

### 5.2.4 An Overview of New Zealand's Economic Reform and Its Future

It is apparent that the process of change in New Zealand has caused considerable disruption among specific sectors of the economy, particularly those that enjoyed monopolistic profits thanks to high levels of protectionism and isolation from domestic and/or foreign competition.

Four questions are raised when such changes take place in any economy: first, are the benefits worth the cost of reform? Second, what reforms matter most? Third, how are reforms conducted? And finally, what are the next steps after such changes? (Prebble 1994).

First, it is very difficult to calculate all the benefits and costs of any economic reform, simply because people's perceptions and behaviors change continuously, as they adjust to new economic scenarios. But some New Zealand's economic results are particularly interesting.

Inflation has come down dramatically from close to 20% in the early 1980's to less than 2% in the mid 1990's. Obviously, New Zealand is not alone in enjoying low rates of inflation in the last few years. However, the magnitude of New Zealand's improvement is very impressive in that they went from being the highest inflation country among the OECD members to the lowest one. This relative improvement cannot be attributed only to deflationary pressures around the globe, and is clearly proof of success against inflationary pressures in New Zealand's reform process.

Economic growth is another benchmark used to measure the activity of an economy. During the beginning of the reform process New Zealand suffered years of very slow growth and even several years of recession. However, it has enjoyed growth figures of 2% to 3% since 1991 with an impressive 5.3% growth rate in 1994. These numbers by no means represent an economic boom, but are quite impressive compared with most of the developed countries which are just recovering from recessions (with the exception of the U.S.). Moreover, the fact that New Zealand has enjoyed positive growth rates over the last few years without fiscal or monetary expansion must be another sign of successful reforms.

Export growth has probably been the main driving force behind this expansion. This is not the result of an improvement in prices of agricultural commodities, but rather it represents real expansion in a wide range of products with new sales of new products into new markets. The growing products include timber and computer software, thus penetrating new niche-markets around the globe. Furthermore, the range of markets has widened from mainly one country, Great Britain, to several nations including Australia, U.S., Japan, Great Britain, Taiwan, South Korea, Germany, etc. This diversification and expansion of exports is a sign of new flexibility and increased productivity which translates into competitiveness in many markets. This also may be attributed in part to the reform process.

Overall, the process of change has been painful for many people, but a changed vibrant economy is emerging in the midst of greater uncertainty for many. The fact that New Zealanders are now less complacent about the future may be seen in itself as one of the success stories of the reform process.

Secondly, it is even more difficult to exclude the successful specific changes of the reform process since most of them are complementary of each other. Still, those of special importance will be pointed out.

The independence of the central bank, clear monetary policy, and credibility in the fight against inflation has reduced many uncertainties and has increased incentives for future investments. Other countries have managed to achieve similar results in inflation without New Zealand's institutional arrangements; therefore, it is not suggested here this is the only way to prevent inflation, but obviously it has worked for New Zealand.

The reform of government management through greater emphasis on accountability and responsibility has put in place better specified incentives and has identified specific goals which are leading to a tighter and more efficient government. The abandonment of protectionist policies and the adoption of freer trade with Australia and the APEC countries through specific trade agreements has allowed for increased competition, thus forcing changes in the old habits of production and distribution.

The labor market reforms have introduced a new industrial relations system. The old systems of national wage bargaining and compulsory union membership became the major causes of New Zealand's labor market inflexibility. The new arrangement of enterprise bargaining has presented a new window of flexibility in the labor market with productivity improvements in many sectors of the economy.

All of the above, along with the government's consistent micro-economic focus addressing the incentives of economic agents in the economy, has permitted the design of new and clear policies for the New Zealanders to understand, to debate, and to support.

Thirdly, these reforms were conducted and implemented thanks to the specific characteristics of the society and the circumstances facing the nation at that particular time in the early 1980's.

New Zealand was and still is relatively a young and small country, particularly compared to some Western European nations. Both of these characteristics have allowed for the so-called "Pragmatic Kiwi," or a spirit of radicalism and practicality to inspire debate and change.

By 1984 New Zealand was at the brink of economic chaos with massive twin deficits, high inflation, and loss of confidence in its currency affecting everyone in New Zealand, including significant lobbying groups such as the New Zealand Federated Farmers. Soon after, they advocated an anti-inflation policy suggesting the removal of farm subsidies with the immediate support of the government and influential business people. Everybody began to advocate change, and thus the need for change became apparent even to the laymen and women of New Zealand.

This needed change sought by all New Zealanders was characterized by consultation. The government outlined policy reforms and asked for feedback on specific issues from its people. This process allowed the government access to expertise in many different areas. This process of consultation also reduced uncertainty and fear on the part the public, resolved many technical concerns from the professionals, and stimulated debate and consensus among all parties. Moreover, the government passed a new law where any information, unless there were specific legal reasons to withhold the information, had to be disclosed to the public on request. The government has and still is working toward a closer relationship between the public and the private sector, and the public mistrust toward public officials seems to have decreased as a result.

And finally, the next steps in New Zealand's journey of structural and economic reforms are by no means finished, but the expectation that radical reforms will continue are past.

Obviously, the opposition parties want to alter some of the policies that have taken effect over the last few years, but there is not expected to be a sudden reversal of direction.

Two major areas of change are fiscal and social policy. On the fiscal side, the total government debt being over 60% of GDP as of 1991 is a big concern, and there is growing consensus that a reduction of the domestic as well as the foreign debt is necessary to stay and to sustain the path of economic growth[100]. On the social side, the Maori indigenous of New Zealand point out that their rights of holding land and other assets under the treaty of Waitangi have been violated; therefore, the government is reconsidering the Maori Land Rights (Prebble 1994, p. 61).

In conclusion, one of the basic elements of this emerging new economy is its linkages with other countries and its increased trade with new partners. Another is its increased domestic investment and the renewed optimism of foreign investors. New Zealand's globalization and institutionally specific strategies of more trade focus, specialization in niche-market goods, involvement indirect overseas businesses, strategic management of its currency, economic integration, flexibility, macro-organizational strategies, and corporatism, have all played an important role in this major economic success story, and will foster continued sustainable economic growth.

### 5.2.5 Testing Propositions and Empirical Results[101]

There are two primary issues being analyzed globalization and institutional strategies of New Zealand, a small open economy, compared to its larger counterpart of Australia. The following sections will examine each proposition by comparing their statistical significance.

Again, this is done to capture the fundamental concept that the size of a nation *does matter* in the internationalization and structural workings of New Zealand from the mid 1980's to 1992.

### *5.2.5.1 Globalization Propositions*

*Proposition One (Trade Focus)* Trade has long been known as an engine of growth for New Zealand, especially in its early development. The mean of New Zealand's trade ratio is .46, almost double that of Australia's .26.

The predicted statistical relationship was found between the trade ratios of New Zealand and Australia; therefore, nation size seems to matter when it comes to trade (see Figure 5–1, Appendix 5–1 and 5–2).

**Figure 5–1. Trade (export-import) Focus**

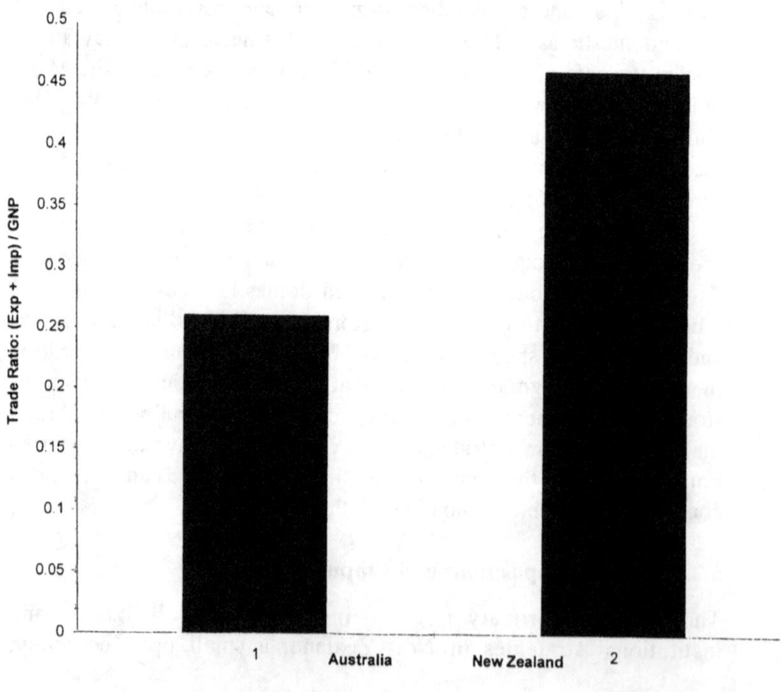

*Note:* Data extracted from the World Bank Tables (1994) from 1985 to 1992. The graph depicts the average of New Zealand and Australia's trade ratios for the 1985–1992 period.

*Proposition Two (Specialization in niche market goods).* New Zealand's manufactures exports are still in the early stages of specialization in order to reach world "niche-market" goods, with the exception of the software industry. The mean of New Zealand's trade manufactures ratio is .0575, significantly higher than that of Australia's .035.

The predicted statistical relationship was thus found between the trade manufactures ratios of New Zealand and Australia; therefore, nation size appears to matter when it comes to trade and concentration of manufactured products in niche markets (see Figure 5–2, Appendix 5–1 and 5–3).

**Figure 5–2. "Niche Market" Goods Specialization**

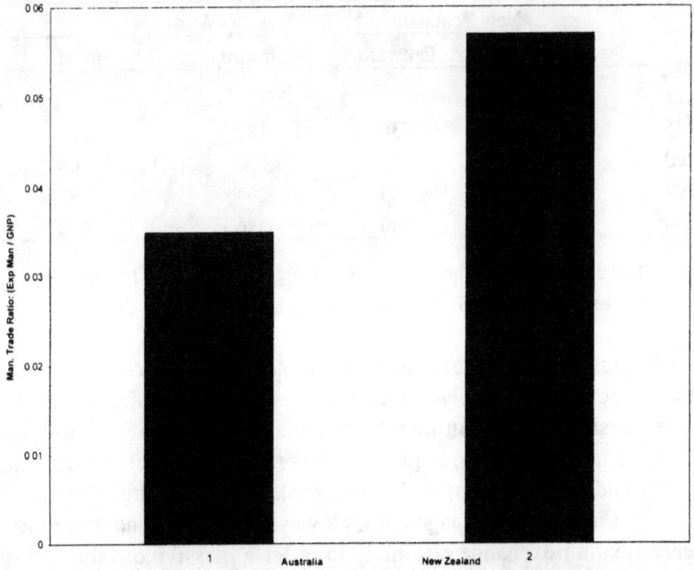


*Note:* Data obtained from the World Bank tables (1994) from 1985 to 1992. The graph illustrates the average of New Zealand and Australia's trade manufactures ratios for the 985–1992 period.

*Proposition Three (Involvement in direct overseas businesses).* Big MNCs from small economies have greater direct business links, especially in FDI, than their larger counterparts. It is a fact that the presence of British multinationals has been a regular phenomenon in New Zealand since its discovery. Moreover, Australia has become a key player in inward FDI to New Zealand since the major re-structuring of the country beginning in 1985. In contrast, New Zealand has also become more involved in investing overseas, particularly in Australia, with almost $NZ 4,000 million in 1990 (Akoorie 1994).

The mean of New Zealand's inward-FDI is .115, smaller than that of Australia's .216. Moreover, the mean of New Zealand and Australia's outward-FDI ratio is the same .08. Obviously, the predicted statistical relationship was not found between inward and outward FDI ratios among these two nations[102] (see Table 5–3).

**Table 5–3. International Business (FDI Focus): 1985–92**

| | FDI Ratio | | | |
|---|---|---|---|---|
| | New Zealand | | Australia | |
| | Inward | Outward | Inward | Outward |
| Year | | | | |
| 1985 | .091 | .036 | .135 | .036 |
| 1990 | .116 | .102 | .250 | .108 |
| 1992 | .137 | .103 | .264 | .097 |
| Mean | .115 | .080 | .216 | .080 |

*Note:* Data extracted from the World Investment Report (1994) for the available years of 1985, 1990, and 1992.

*Proposition Four (Strategic management and use of exchange rates).* The more "globally oriented" a nation like New Zealand is, the more sensitively and strategically it has to manage and use the exchange rate mechanism to price its exports competitively. During the 1970's and early 1980's, both New Zealand and Australia operated pegged or managed exchange rates. However, New Zealand moved to a freely floating exchange rate in 1985, after a massive devaluation of 20% of its currency in 1984 (Sherwin 1990).

Starting from the period of 1973 to 1992, the prediction of New Zealand's need of a larger real depreciation than its larger counterpart of Australia to weather the first oil crisis of 1973 was found to exist.

For example, the nominal exchange rate for New Zealand depreciated 64 percent, but its real exchange rate depreciated almost 85 percent.

In contrast, Australia's nominal depreciation was a little over 50 percent, with a real exchange rate depreciation of around 70 percent. Furthermore, from the beginning of the structural changes in New Zealand in 1985 to 1992, the prediction of the small nation's necessity of a larger real depreciation than its larger counterpart of Australia was found as well. For example, the nominal exchange rate for New Zealand actually appreciated 3.17 percent, but its real exchange rate depreciated 18.94 percent. In contrast, Australia's nominal appreciation was only 1.13 percent, with a real exchange rate depreciation of only 7.80 percent (see Table 5–4).

**Table 5–4. Strategic Management of Exchange Rates:1973–92**

| Nation | Nominal Exchange Rate | Real Exchange Rate |
|---|---|---|
| New Zealand | -64 | -84.40 |
| Australia | -53.72 | -69.80 |

*Source:* International Financial Statistics (1993 & 1994)

**Table 5–5. Strategic Management of Exchange Rates:1985–92**

| Nation | Nominal Exchange Rate | Real Exchange Rate |
|---|---|---|
| New Zealand | +3.17 | -18.94 |
| Australia | +1.13 | -7.80 |

*Source:* International Financial Statistics (1993 & 1994)

*Proposition Five (Price Stability).* Small nations under a truly flexible exchange rate, like New Zealand, tend to better manage inflationary pressures than their larger counterparts. The inflation rates for both, New Zealand and Australia were 7.3 and 5.9 percent respectively.

The predicted statistical significance was not found between the inflation rates of these two nations during the period of 1985 to 1992. This is not surprising due to the fact that New Zealand was experiencing inflation rates of almost 20 percent during the early and mid 1980's while Australia's inflation rates were between 7 and 8 percent during the same period[103]. Furthermore, it is remarkable that New Zealand's was able to reduce inflation to under 2 percent in the early 1990's while enjoying an economic growth rate of around 5 percent per year (see Table 5–6 and Appendix 5–4).

**Table 5–6. Inflation Rates:1985–92**

| Year | New Zealand | Australia |
|---|---|---|
| 1985 | — | — |
| 1986 | 18.23 | 7.38 |
| 1987 | 11.73 | 7.41 |
| 1988 | 8.30 | 8.70 |
| 1989 | 6.18 | 5.80 |
| 1990 | 2.96 | 2.96 |
| 1991 | 1.44 | 1.35 |
| 1992 | 2.16 | .92 |
| Mean | 7.30 | 5.90 |

*Source:* World Bank Tables (1994)

*Proposition Six (International economic integration).* Small nations must engage in trade through varying degrees of economic integration to eliminate size disadvantages, and New Zealand is no exception. The cost of economic isolation became too large for New Zealand in the early 1980's, which led to the Australia New Zealand Closer Economic Relations Treaty with the provision to become a free trade area in 1995.

Thus, New Zealand's market has been expanded more than five times its domestic size, which possibly will diminish its size disadvantages by reaping the economic gains of product differentiation, scale economies, increased competition, and increased bargaining power perhaps within APEC.

### *5.2.5.2 Institutional propositions*

*Proposition Seven (Flexibility).* Small nations must be flexible to endure and to adapt to economic adversity and negative external shocks. New Zealand found its best ally in the government elected in 1984, which quickly raised its degree of flexibility. New Zealand's flexibility mean is 6.3, higher than that of Australia's 4.7.

The predicted statistical significance was surprisingly not found between the degree of flexibility among the two nations[104]. Moreover, the predicted statistical significance would be found assuming equal variances for both nations. Thus, nation size appears to matter when it comes to flexibility (see Appendix 5–5 and 5–6).

*Proposition Eight (Government-Firm complementary relationship).* Governments of small nations do play a very important role in the efficient allocation of their economic resources within their economies, in particular New Zealand's government in its process of economic and structural changes of its economy. The government has indeed strengthened public and private complementary relationships through its many reforms in the goods, labor, and capital markets. The mean of New Zealand's macro-organizational effectiveness is 5.6, somewhat higher than that of Australia's 4.1.

The predicted statistical significance was surprisingly not found between the macro-organizational strategies' effectiveness of the two nations, especially after New Zealand's remarkable economic turnaround. In this case, nation size appears not to matter when it comes to the effectiveness of macro-organizational strategies[105] (see Appendix 5–5 and 5–6).

*Proposition Nine (Corporatism).* Small nations usually show a strong degree of corporatism in regard to macro-economic policy management dealing with wage differentials and the working class, and most importantly yielding a more egalitarian and centralized macro-structure of interest groups. But surprisingly, this is not the case for New Zealand. Some of New Zealand's economic troubles were provoked by years of procrastination and lack of compromise at all levels. The mean of New Zealand's degree of corporatism is 4.6, lower than that of Australia's 5.8.

The predicted statistical significance was of course not found among the degree of corporatism of both countries. Thus, nation size seems not to matter when it comes to corporatism when comparing New Zealand and Australia[106] (see Appendix 5–5 and 5–6).

### *5.2.5.3 Regression Analysis*

Due to the importance of exports and FDI as the main engines of economic growth for New Zealand, GNP is regressed on exports, export manufactures, but not on FDI since the statistical results of section 5.2.5.1 are not significant. As with any linear regression exercise, the results should be interpreted with caution since important variables may not be fully captured

Repeatedly, the greater importance of exports and export manufactures is observed in New Zealand compared to its larger counterpart of Australia, in order to explain changes in GNP. The coefficient estimates were higher both for exports 1.49 and export manufactures 4.9 in New Zealand as compared with Australia, whose coefficient estimates were .36 and .60 respectively. This reveals the significance of international trade in New Zealand to help it overcome smallness and secure economic growth. All regressions exhibit $R^2$s of .90 or higher. These results substantiate those obtained previously while testing the globalization propositions (see Table 5–7).

**Table 5–7. New Zealand. Regression Analysis (1985–92)**

| | Coefficient estimates (t-statistics) | R square |
|---|---|---|
| New Zealand | | |
| Export | 1.49 | .9503 |
| | (10.72) | |
| Exman | 4.99 | .9292 |
| | (8.08) | |
| Australia | | |
| Export | .3609 | .9735 |
| | (14.86) | |
| Exman | .6020 | .9762 |
| | (15.69) | |

## 5.3 SUMMARY

This chapter has provided two case studies: Catalonia, a regional study, and New Zealand, a country case.

The first part of the chapter examined the Catalonia case study first by presenting factual evidence of the globalization strategies and the institutional structure of the region, and second by supporting the concept that the region size within a country still does matter in international trade, especially in the globalization efforts of Catalonia. In addition, region size also does matter when dealing with the flexibility and institutional characteristics of Catalonia.

The latter part of the chapter examined the New Zealand case study presenting empirical evidence to support the concept that nation size does matter in international trade, especially in the globalization efforts of New Zealand, compared to its larger counterpart of Australia.

In contrast, the results did not present much evidence to support the idea that nation size does matter when dealing with the flexibility and institutional characteristics of New Zealand, compared to its larger counterpart of Australia

### Appendix 5–1. Trade & Trade Manufactures Ratio

| Nation | Trade | Trade Manuf. |
|---|---|---|
| New Zealand | .46 | .057 |
| Australia | .26 | .035 |

*Source*: World Bank Tables (1994).

### Appendix 5–2. Trade Focus

| | | Univariate procedure | |
|---|---|---|---|
| Nation | Mean (%) | Variance | Std. Dev. |
| New Zealand | .461 | .00138 | .0372 |
| Australia | .264 | .00020 | .0141 |

| | T-Test procedure | |
|---|---|---|
| Variances | T Prob > | T |
| Unequal | -14.04 | .0001 |
| Equal | -14.04 | .0001 |
| F' | 6.98 | .0201 |

### Appendix 5–3. Trade Manufactures Focus

| | | Univariate procedure | |
|---|---|---|---|
| Nation | Mean (%) | Variance | Std. Dev. |
| New Zealand | .057 | .000025 | .005 |
| Australia | .035 | .000167 | .013 |

| | T-Test procedure | |
|---|---|---|
| Variances | T Prob > | T |
| Unequal | -3.25 | .0333 |
| Equal | -3.25 | .0175 |
| F' | 6.67 | .1535 |

## Appendix 5–4. Price Stability-Inflation Rates

| | | Univariate procedure | |
|---|---|---|---|
| Nation | Mean (%) | Variance | Std. Dev. |
| New Zealand | 7.27 | 36.76 | 6.063 |
| Australia | 4.91 | 10.12 | 3.181 |

| | | T-Test procedure |
|---|---|---|
| Variances | T Prob > | T |
| Unequal | -.91 | .3859 |
| Equal | -.91 | .3803 |
| F' | 3.63 | .1416 |

## Appendix 5–5. Flexibility, Macro-Organizational, and Corporatism Ratings

| Nation | Flexibility | Macro-Organization | Corporatism |
|---|---|---|---|
| New Zealand | 6.27 | 5.62 | 4.60 |
| Australia | 4.66 | 4.14 | \5.82 |

*Source*: The World Competitiveness Report (1992–1994).

## Appendix 5–6. Flexibility, Macro-Organizational, and Corporatism Focus

| Flexibility | | Univariate procedure | |
|---|---|---|---|
| Nation | Mean | Variance | Std. Dev. |
| New Zealand | 6.27 | .4522 | .6725 |
| Australia | 4.66 | .8472 | .9204 |
| Macro-Organiz. Strategy | | | |
| Nation | | | |
| New Zealand | 5.62 | 4.58 | 2.14 |
| Australia | 4.14 | 1.97 | 1.40 |
| Corporatism | | | |
| Nation | | | |
| New Zealand | 4.60 | 1.83 | 1.35 |
| Australia | 5.82 | .21 | .460 |

**Appendix 5–6.** *(continued)*

| | T-Test procedure | |
|---|---|---|
| | T Prob > | T |
| Flexibilty | | |
| Variances | | |
| Unequal | -2.43 | .1352 |
| Equal | -2.43 (() | .0715 |
| F' | 1.87 | .6960 |
| Macro-Organiz. | | |
| Strategy | | |
| Variances | | |
| Unequal | -1.003 | .4213 |
| Equal | -1.003 | .3724 |
| F' | 2.23 | .6015 |
| Corporatism | | |
| Variances | | |
| Unequal | 1.48 | .2760 |
| Equal | 1.48 | .2118 |
| F' | 8.64 | .2076 |

CHAPTER 6

# Concluding Remarks

The purpose of this study has been to provide a more comprehensive measurement of smallness than conventional for the analysis of the globalization strategies and structural adaptability of nations to overcome smallness and to secure economic growth. The central issue involved in this book is whether existing or new small independent economic units, once created out of national disintegration, can survive and prosper with their own limited domestic market.

In developing a comprehensive study of nation size, outward orientation, and structural adaptability, this study has not been simply an intellectual exercise, rather it has attempted to develop an in-depth understanding of small independent economic units within the European Union so that proper policy decisions can be made in the future. Also, this book has presented a region and a country case study on Catalonia and New Zealand respectively.

The main hypothesis developed in this study is that the size of a nation matters in international trade and structural adaptability as a determinant of economic viability; particularly in this new global economic environment where the number of nations has almost doubled in the last half century, to close to 200 independent states. This has been done by looking at the macroeconomic factors which have caused small nations to expand domestic markets and to adapt their institutions.

It has been hypothesized that small economies, compared to their larger counterparts, when economically successful tend to be (1) more export focused in manufacturing, particularly in early stages of development; (2) likely to specialize in differentiated manufactures as they advance in industrialization; (3) more actively involved with direct overseas businesses; (4) more sensitive in strategically managing exchange rates as a macroeconomic instrument of competitiveness for its firms; (5) likely to be in a better position to achieve price stability and; (6) more actively involved in international trade through varying degrees of economic integration. In other words, small countries are more "globalized" in terms of the above measures of exploiting the opportunities in the global economy.

Additionally, international competitiveness, to some degree, is a matter of institutional flexibility and macro-corporatism. Then, it is also hypothesized that small economies, compared to their larger counterparts, tend to present (1) a higher degree of flexibility; (2) greater likelihood to forge the complementary government/firm relationship necessary for the XXI century, and (3) a higher degree of corporatism allowing for greater consensus and effectiveness in macro-economic policy management. In other words, small nations are more "flexible" in terms of the above measures in adapting to external changing economic conditions.

The two hypothesis of the book were supported by the empirical evidence presented in Chapter 4 and 5. The importance of trade and flexibility was demonstrated in the estimated regressions and T-Test which showed, for the most part, significant results existing between nation size and the 9 propositions set forth.

The information provided by inflation, however, showed an expected unimportant correlation, and the results provided by the macro-organizational effectiveness showed an unexpected unimportant correlation in the European Union. The impact of global and sometimes unknown domestic variables can be difficult to identify, thus impacting the outcome of the statistical analysis.

Furthermore, the information provided by FDI and price stability showed an unexpected relatively unimportant relationship in the case of New Zealand when compared to its larger counterpart of Australia. And finally, the New Zealand results' of all structural propositions showed a surprising insignificant correlation, when compared to Australia.

It becomes extremely important for the researcher to keep in mind that it is difficult to capture all the parametric factors occurring worldwide in a two-variable regression analysis or a simple t-test. Thus anyone must be careful with the interpretations of the analysis presented here and always use economic intuition taking into account the impact of local and global economic conditions. This is not to negate any of the empirical findings, but rather to establish the importance of small economic units in the light of past economic history and present global economic conditions.

This study, including the discussion in this chapter, points to the importance of understanding the economic viability of small independent states, since they are becoming more numerous and smaller and more important. If separatists continue demanding secession and independence (i.e. Canada, Sri Lanka, and Spain), they need to anticipate smallness effects as carefully as possible and be ready to adapt as needed. By remaining fixed on the idea that small nations can do just fine by overlooking outward orientation and structural adaptability, these nations may miss the opportunity to become economically successful as the world continues to integrate economically.

It is interesting to note that conditions worldwide are changing very rapidly in part from the break-up of the former Soviet bloc into a large number of small independent nations in Central and Eastern Europe, with the continuing threat of even further subdivision within this region. Moreover, Canada has been confronted with the possibility of Quebec's secession.

This all points to the importance of developing specific approaches to outward orientation and structural adaptability to overcome smallness and secure economic growth for the already existing and newly formed small independent states. Hopefully, this book will provide some guidance from which future domestic and international economic policy decisions can be made, decisions which will have a positive impact upon the economic viability of small countries as the global economy continues to grow while the size of the parts continues to shrink.

# Notes

1. There exists a study group called SMOPEC (small open economies) comprised of approximately 25 scholars from various nationalities, most of whom are European. These are some of the members: Aharoni, Castello, and Ozawa (U.S.A.), Beer and Bellak (Austria), Gaertner and Oxelheim (Sweden), Hirsch (Israel), Luostarinen (Finland), Davis, Pedersen, and Thomsen (Denmark), Simoes (Portugal), Magnusson (Iceland), Jaklic, Rojec, and Svetlicic (Slovenia). The initiative for cooperation on SMOPECs got started within the EIBA conference in Lisbon in 1993. The first official meeting of scholars interested in SMOPEC affairs was in Vienna, Austria in 1994. A second meeting was held during the EIBA conference in Urbino, Italy in December of 1995.

2. See Wall Street Journal (June 20, 1994) article: "Global Paradox, growth of trade binds nations, but it also can spur separatism." Paul Goble, a specialist in ethnic movements at the Carnegie Endowment for International Peace, believes that the world may fracture into 500 states from the nearly 200.

3. Becker (1990) starts his magazine article by saying: "When separatists in Quebec, Lithuania, Ethiopia, Sri Lanka, Spain, and elsewhere demand secession and independence, they are often accused of encouraging the formation of states that are too small to be economically viable. But it is not all clear that on balance large countries have decisive economic advantages. . . . Indeed, countries with either bigger populations or larger areas tend to have slightly lower per capita incomes than smaller countries."

4. Other explanations have to be sought in sociological, psychological, and institutional factors rather than in economic ones.

5. According to Olson's theory of collective choice the free-rider problem is less disruptive of collective action of small groups.

6. Olson (1982) views interest groups as having a tendency to outstay their welcome, it seems there is an inertia which prevents those groups from disappearing even if they lose much of their original support and the rationale for their existence

7. We will further explore the higher degree of corporatism shown by small nations, through class compromise, parliamentary alliances, and consensus seeking, particularly the 'Nordic' countries. The 'Nordic economic model' where government strongly assisted in creating, upgrading, and allocating economic resources through specific macro-organizational strategies probably could have not been implemented in a large nation.

8. A strong trade orientation leads to an active engagement in direct overseas operations, both inward and outward. For example, small open economies, in their early stages of development, encourage inward FDI to build domestic productive capacities; they also set up their own overseas marketing facilities via FDI (that is, as complements of trade). They also promote licensing for and investments in local production abroad, especially when they can no longer retain a competitive advantage in home-based production for certain lines of products or when they find it much more cost-effective and profitable to produce abroad (that is, as second best or even superior substitutes for exports).

Furthermore, the more strategically dependent a nation is on trade and direct overseas operations, the greater the role of exchange rates in affecting its economic activities, and the more sensitive the nation naturally becomes to management of the exchange rate regime. In fact, any economy that uses trade as an engine of growth, especially in its early stages of development, needs to prevent, at least, a real appreciation of its currency, but usually to strategically maintain a real depreciation (home currency undervaluation) to have a favorable effect on the current account by keeping its exports somewhat 'subsidized' and its imports 'taxed'.

9. Hirsch and Thomsen (1993) specifically emphasize this point: "Economic activities . . . are not undertaken by countries, but by firms. Firms embody the mechanism which translates the abstract concepts of competitive advantage into marketable goods and services" (p. 237). A distinction between micro and macro elements is also made, though in a somewhat different context, by Bellak (1993). Hirsch and Thomsen's

study explores the patterns of industrialization of industrial firms in Denmark and Israel, two small open economies, on a comparative basis. Bellak's work analyzes the flows of FDI into and out of Austria as a small open economy.

10. In other words, a shift from home-embedded production to overseas production by their own multinationals appears much earlier for small nation firms than their large nation counterparts

11. By the same token, the establishment of a competitive exchange rate ought to be conducive to adaptation providing an incentive and an increase in tradeable goods and a disincentive to buy imports.

12. See Castello and Ozawa's (1994) article presented at the International Trade and Finance Association at Reading, England (July, 13–16, 1994).

13. See Wall Street Journal's article (January, 18, 1995): "In Rival Theories, Technology is the Key." by Bruce Bartlett. He argues that economists are divided into two theoretical camps when explaining economic growth: the exogenous advocating economic growth as a function of *outside* forces, and the endogenous promoting economic growth as a function of forces within the economy.

Joseph Schumpeter argued that economic development was an spontaneous and discontinuous change in the channels of flow, which altered displaced the equilibrium previous existing. For him technological change in the form of invention and innovation was the foundation for modern economic development (the notion of creative destruction).

Exogenous Growth Theory (Harrod, Domar, Solow, and Swan) allows for technological change, but it does not make it an endogenous outcome of profit maximizing behavior of firms who invest in knowledge creation. In the New Growth Theory, (Romer, Grossman, Helpman, Lucas, and Sala i Martin) technology is seen as a result from policies that reward innovation and entrepreneurial risk-taking—thus, technology is no longer consider exogenous.

It is in this innovation and entrepreneurship that small open economies base their creation of dynamic comparative advantages in order to export manufactures, to specialize in "niche market goods," and to promote outward FDI.

14. This section is based upon—and an extension of—Castello and Ozawa (1994).

15. The studies focus on a variety of nations ranging from less developed, developing, semi-industrialized, and industrialized.

Obviously, the results are sometimes contradictory since we are comparing a broad range of nations with completely different markets, institutions, and economic characteristics. Moreover, the statistical techniques used are different too. Given the proposition that for small open economies there exists a stronger relationship between exports and economic growth than for their larger counterparts; therefore, the hypothesis of export-led growth can be strongly supported for smaller economies.

16. Cointegration means that there is a stable long run relationship among the levels of certain economic variables, in our case exports and GNP. Thus, if individual time series are integrated of order one, they may be cointegrated which means that one or more linear combinations of these variables is stationary even though individually they are not. A failure to find cointegration suggests that such variables have no long run link. It does not necessarily mean that there is no stable, long run relationship among the variables, but it does suggest that there is no stable, long run, *linear relationship* among them.

17. Hirsch and Thomsen (1993) posit a substitute relation: "When individual small country firms seek to expand, they soon encounter the constraints imposed by their small domestic markets. They must *choose* between product diversification and market diversification. When they choose the latter, they engage in internationalization" (p. 237). There must be some good reasons for this substitute relation, but unfortunately no explanation is given.

18. For example, Sweden, Finland, and Denmark are traditionally world-renowned for highly differentiated tableware made of silver, steel, glass, china, and earthware (Kindleberger, 1984, p.106).

19. We should point out some of the difficulties measuring FDI. According to Bellak and Luostarinen (1994, p. 10): "FDI data is either based on balance of payments or on information delivered by firms. . . . Balance of payments data exclude investments that were financed from sources abroad. Firm data include exchange rate as well as accounting problems."

20. One important way of producing a real depreciation is to maintain price stability at home; this is especially important if a small nation operates under fixed exchange rates. Are there any structural elements peculiar to small open economies that help stabilize domestic prices (i.e., control inflation)? In other words, are small open economies in a better position to achieve price stability because of their

smallness? This question will be pursued further in an attempt to empirically test some of these hypotheses.

21. We recognize that inflation in Eastern European countries is not the only cause of political instability. There are many other factors (massive monetary hang over) that are beyond the scope of this section.

22. Assuming the following: first, the velocity of money is constant and second quantity is stable.

23. In the short run, an increase in the money supply raises both nominal and real output. But in the long run, employees adjust their nominal wage claims and output is restored to their natural levels. Thus, changes in the money supply affect prices and nominal incomes but not real incomes.

24. Assuming the prices of foreign goods, in terms of their own currencies, are unchanged.

25. Depicted by the Phillips Curve describing an empirical relationship between wage, price inflation, and unemployment. Thus it suggests a trade off between unemployment and inflation (the higher the rate of unemployment, the lower the rate of inflation). Recently, the Phillips Curve has shown a propensity to shift between sloping vertical and horizontal and has been strongly criticized. Thus economists have shown disbelief in this trade off to assist them in predicting future inflationary pressures.

26. See Gros, D. and Thygesen, N. (1992). "Consumer inflation in 12 EC countries had come down from a peak of 15 percent in 1974 to 9.2 percent in 1978. Over the same period, it was reduced in Germany from 7.5 percent to 2.8 percent. . . . Consequently, Germany saw its currency rise steeply." Collignon, Bofinger, Jonhson, and de Maigret (1994, p. 15).

27. In response to speculative movements in 1993, the marginal intervention limits for all currencies participating in the ERM have been widened to +/- 15 percent around their bilateral central rates. Thus, the exchange rate mechanism is still fixed, but very adjustable.

28. There is new evidence of low inflation in Europe. See The Wall Street Journal article, November 21, 1994: "Europe Looks Forward to Era of Low Inflation." Terence Roth writes that in the year ahead, the world can expect more proof that Europe's old inflation bugbear seems to be in hibernation despite an accelerating economic recovery. Moreover, Roger Bootle claims: "The power of trade unions is waning as industry shifts away from basic production. New competitive pressures from cheaper products in Asia and Eastern Europe, plus

deregulation, privatization, corporate streamlining and new fiscal restraint at home, will all help keep price levels down."

29. Economic integration is a process whereby participating economies merge economic and political rules and decision-making institutions to varying degrees. There are five levels of economic integration. In increasing order of further integration, they include: (1) a free trade area (nations abolish trade barriers among members, but each nation retains its own barriers vis-a-vis nonmembers nations, for example the recently signed NAFTA agreement, EFTA, and LAFTA), (2) a customs union (it extends the free trade area by incorporating common external trade barriers between member nations and the rest of the world), (3) a common market (it removes barriers against free flow of the factors of production—e.g., labor and capital—among member nations, for example the EAC), (4) an economic and monetary union (members of a common market adopt a common currency and agree to give a supranatural authority the power to establish harmonious, coordinated monetary and fiscal policy, currently the EU is working toward the completion of this phase of economic integration), and (5) full economic integration (member nations of a monetary union relinquish some individual autonomy and form one government which establishes and integrates the primary political and economic working rules for all members, for example the U.S.A. since the late eighteenth century). (Angresano 1992, p. 355).

30. Successful states in their aspirations to become independent from their central government will not attain full sovereignty, since control of their own jurisdiction will be partially transferred to their new trading partners.

Sovereignty used to be considered the hallmark of a country, but today even large powerful nations have added many external constraints with the increasing importance of trade within their economies that the concept of sovereignty is becoming archaic.

31. In Chapter Six, special attention will be devoted to the specific case of Catalonia wanting independence from Spain. If successful, Catalonia could become another small open economy in Western Europe applying for membership in the European Union.

32. A major obstacle for the UK to join the EC was the adoption of a common agricultural policy and the eventual political unity of Western Europe which were in direct conflict with the UK's interests in the Commonwealth. Even to this day the British are not very cooperative in pursuing the EU's objectives.

33. With the exceptions of the ASEAN-Association of South-East Asian Nations-and the LAFTA-Latin American Free Trade Area-economic agreements.

34. Dunning (1992, p. 8) defines macro-organizational strategies as: "the actions taken by governments to optimize the modality by which the resources and capabilities within their jurisdictions are created, upgraded and allocated among different uses, and the efficiency at which these are deployed for any given use."

35. Dunning (1992) suggests that this economic interdependence by the small nations, especially within the European Union, will not only add a new dimension to their domestic macro-economic policy; but if these nations expect huge gains from economic integration, their institutions must be flexible to adjust to be in line with those of the countries with which they trade.

36. Dominique Strauss-Kahn, former French Minister for Industry and Foreign Trade, writes: "Competitiveness no longer pertains merely to the corporate world acting in isolation, rather, it involves the entire economy. . . . Government must become a full-fledged economic partner, its main role being one of mediator: to stimulate research and multiply the links between research and industry, to support emerging technologies, to bring companies closer together. . . ." (World Competitiveness Report 1993, p. 274).

37. Small open economies are in fact more flexible than their larger counterparts and therefore are in a better position to achieve such an objective.

38. Since it is the primary sector of most small open economies.

39. For example, the Dutch government stimulated in the past R&D in the industry by: the 'Innovation Stimulating Arrangement' and a 'Technology Development Credit Regulation.' Recently, specific incentives include the participation in research programs of the European Union. Also, new funds have been set aside to support high tech companies like telecommunication systems, semiconductors, and software and systems development. (World Competitiveness Report 1993, p. 290–293).

40. For further detail see Schimitter (1981, p. 293–294). He uses two measures of corporatism based on the degree of organizational centralization and representational monopoly of trade unions. Other measures used are based on the degree of institutionalized participation in policy making and the commitment to social partnership by trade

unions and their leaders.See also Katzenstein (1985), Grant (1985), Williamson (1989), and Henley and Tsakalotos (1993).

41. Williamson (1989) ranks corporatism into three different categories—strong, medium, and weak. He also measures corporatism based on organizational centralization, and the extent to which a single national association enjoys a representational monopoly. In other words, a high degree of corporatism can be observed where trade union organizations are highly centralized and monopolistic.

42. However, there might be room for accommodating exchange rate movements: first, to help reduce uncertainty about future profit levels and encourage investments, and second, to reduce the effect of unsustainable nominal wage increases.

43. Sweden which joined the European Union effective January 1, 1995, plans to increase taxes to finance the country's EU membership payments due in 1998. The ministry already has parliamentary support for increasing taxes on commercial and farm property, vehicle emissions, and utilities. According to "The Economist" (January 14, 1995) in the article entitled "Sweden: Personna Grata," Sweden unveiled the 1995–1996 budget, announcing tax rises and spending cuts, while preserving the world's most lavish welfare state and egalitarian style.

44. These principles were first, the elimination of internal barriers to trade; second, the achievement of a customs union; third, the establishment of a common market; and finally, the realization of further integration.

45. According to "The Economist" (August 5th, 1995, p. 96) Ireland, a small economy, is the fastest growing economy in the European Union with GDP rising by more than 5% in 1994."Ireland will grow by around 5% both this year and in 1996. . . . The 10% devaluation of the Irish pound in early 1993 removed pressure on interest rates and the exchange rate." Moreover, Ireland has been able to keep inflation in check with consumer prices rising only 2.4% last year, well belowthe average of industrialized nations.

46. Once again, technology is being emphasized by the New Growth Theory as a main engine of economic growth.

47. The real exchange rate of the home-currency price of $ is measured in terms of DM/$ or Pesetas/$. For example, the real DM/$ exchange rate can be interpreted as the DM needed to pay for one dollar times the price ratio between the two countries ($P_{Germany} / P_{U.S.}$).

48. Furthermore, the European Union is contemplating the admission of 15 more countries which have already applied, application is expected soon, or intend to apply in the future.

49. All regressions and statistical analysis were run using the software package, SAS.

50. This section is based on the 'Dummy Variable Model' of Griffiths, Hill, and Judge (1993, Chapter 17).

51. LM uses the method of least squares to fit general linear models. During processing, GLM groups the dependent variables on their missing values across observations so that sums and cross-products can be collected in the most efficient manner.

52. Those countries joining after 1973 will be represented with time series data only from the year of their membership in the European Union. These countries include Spain, Portugal, and Greece. Austria, Finland, and Sweden will not be included in the analysis, since their membership took effect January 1st, 1995.

53. The T-statistic significance levels are at the 90 percent or above.

54. Two case studies, the Catalonian case within European Union boundaries, and the New Zealand case outside European boundaries will also be analyzed. These will be further developed in the next chapter.

55. The hypothesis that the means of the two groups of observations are equal can be rejected.

56. The hypothesis that the means of the two groups of observations are equal cannot be rejected. The lack of data and the insufficient number of degrees of freedom can be the cause of the insignificance of the statistical results.

57. It is important to point out during the 1973–1992 period, Germany and four small nations, the Netherlands, Belgium, Luxembourg, and Austria experienced nominal and real appreciations of their currencies. As the PPP predicts, perhaps high inflation large countries tended to have weaker currencies in nominal terms than their low inflation small neighbors.

58. If we were to exclude Portugal and Greece from the small sample group, the inflation rate of small economies drops to 6.13 percent, but it is still not statistically significant. Thus the hypothesis that the inflation rate means of small and large nations are equal cannot be rejected.

59. These are the Czech Republic, Slovakia, Hungary, Estonia, Latvia, Lithuania, Slovenia, Bulgaria, and Romania.

60. See "The Economist" (May 13th, 1995, p. 14) for the specifics to be eligible to membership of the world's foremost economic club. At its Copenhagen summit in 1993, the EU announced that to be eligible a country must have first, stable institutions; second, democracy and the rule of law; third, respect human rights and protect minorities; and finally, a functioning market economy to survive the rigors of the single market.

61. See "The Economist"(March 26th, 1994, p. 58)

62. The Survey is conducted annually as a fundamental part of the Report, which includes a 122 item questionnaire sent to 10,300 executives in top and middle management with usually a response rate of 25 percent. The scale of the Scoreboard, one to ten, is calculated according to standard deviation values assuming a default weight of one for each criterion (ten being the highest).

63. FDI figures were only reported in 5–year averages, thus we used data from 1980, 1985, 1990, and 1992.

64. Data collection for countries that joined the European Union later than 1973 such as Greece, Portugal, and Spain begin in the year of their inception. Austria, Finland, and Sweden's inflation rate were 4.7, 3.2, and 3.1 percent respectively in 1992.

65. See the article: "New Zealand success story" in 'The Economist' July 9th, 1994 for further detail.

66. See for further detail the Wall Street Journal article (December 14, 1994): "Kiwi School of Economics."

67. The Catalan parliament is composed of 135 deputies for a period of four years. This implies approval of the president's program of government and of his executive cabinet of twelve ministers responsible for the various areas of government devolved under the statute.

68. The supreme body of government of the region with areas of competence in home office matters, economy and finance, education, culture, health and social security, public works, agriculture, industry and energy, and trade and tourism.

69. The Economist (January 14, 1995) in the article: "Spain: Festering," reports: "The Catalan nationalists, who have kept him (Prime Minister Felipe Gonzalez) in power since he lost his overall majority in the June 1993 general election, continue to prop him up.

70. Boyd (1988, p. 228) writes: "Catalonia, incidentally, is the only non-nation state to have its flag on the moon along with those of the United Nations. The curious reason for this is that the nuclear physicist Werner von Braun was born in Catalonia and insisted on it."

71. The statistics and data that appeared in this section are drawn from two sources; first, Lleonart (1992): *Catalonia: A Land and Economy*, a joint economic study published by the Department of Commerce, Consumption and Tourism of the Generalitat of Catalonia and the Official Chamber of Commerce, Industry and Navigation of Barcelona. And second, Puig i Bastard (1990): *Atlas Comercial de Catalunya*, a project published by the Official Chamber of Commerce, Industry and Navigation of Barcelona.

72. It is important to notice that the Catalan economy enjoyed such tremendous growth thanks largely to the selection of Barcelona, the capital of Catalonia, as host of the 1992 Summer Olympic games; thus, accelerating the creation of infrastructure in the city and the rest of the region.

73. These are the top ten multinational corporations in Catalonia based on sales which provide more than 50,000 jobs to the region: (1) Volkswagen, (2) Nissan, (3) Bayer, (4) Nestle, (5) Hoechst, (6) Sony, (7) BSN, (8) Henkel, (9) Philips, and (10) Siemens.

74. Catalonia is an important European tourist region with cliffs and sandy beaches, marinas, sky resorts, golf courses, and theme parks; therefore, attracting some 14 million tourists from all over Europe and the rest of the world every year.

75. Catalonia is the Spanish Autonomous Community most opened to the global market place. It represents 25% of all Spanish exports and more than 30% of imports.

76. Catalonia's concentration of foreign commerce with France is depicted by its almost 20% of total exports directed toward French territory.

77. In 1991, Catalonia absorbed 43% of total inward FDI in Spain, being the most dynamic autonomous community in this area. There are more than 5,000 Catalan enterprises with participation of foreign capital.

78. German companies from the automobile, chemical, and pharmaceutical sectors are the main investors, although they often make FDIs through their subsidiaries in the Netherlands or Switzerland. Other country sources of FDI are Britain, Belgium, Luxembourg, Italy,

Sweden, Finland, Denmark, Ireland, United States, Canada, Australia, Kuwait, and Venezuela.

Furthermore, Japanese FDI has been increasing since the 1970's when Japanese companies began (for example KAO) to establish themselves using Catalonia as one of their platforms for entering European markets. Since the Single European Market of 1993, there has been a surge of Japanese firms acquiring Catalan companies in order to not be left out the huge European market. Presently, 85% of the industrial investment of Japan in Spain is concentrated in Catalonia with more than 120 Japanese companies employing 15,000 workers.

79. Catalonia has traditionally paid great attention to culture and the fostering of new ideas, not only in humanities but also in the technical and scientific field. Catalan natives have been internationally recognized in the fields of painting and sculpture (Salvador Dali, and Antonio Tapies); architecture (Antonio Gaudi, and Ricard Bofill); music (Pau Casals, Montserrat Caballe, and Josep Carreras); literature (Salvador Espriu, and Josep Pla); and science (Antoni Puigvert, Joan Oro, and Bosch Gimpera).

80. Although 30% of the population was born outside the territory, only a minority do not understand the language.

81. The travel distance by car along the Mediterranean Sea from North to South is less than four hours.

82. 44 million tons of goods were moved by the Catalan port system in 1991.

83. Currently, Catalonia has numerous research centers such as: Mathematics Research Center, National Microelectronics Center, Center for Industrial Laser Applications, Institute for the Science of Materials, Chemical Institute of Sarria, Cybernetics Institute, Scientific Research Council, and many others.

84. "The Economist" survey on cities (July 29th, 1995) refers to cities being transformed with special mention of Barcelona showing how it is possible to transform a city from top to toe. The article reads as follow: "In the mid 1970's, the Mediterranean port was much like any other run-down industrial city in Europe. Its factories were closing, its middle class were living. Two decades and more than 1,000 public-sector construction projects later, Barcelona is thriving. . . . The city's fabric, though left substantially intact, has been embellished with hundreds of small new projects.

It has not come cheap: 12% of the city's budget goes on public investment, and local taxes in the city are about twice what they are in the suburbs. . . . The man who has been mayor during most of the transformation, Pasqual Maragall, has just been re-elected for a fourth term on a promise to increase public investment to 14% of the budget."

85. According to The Economist's article (November 19, 1994): "Estonia: In a Bear's Paw." "Estonia displays a picture of dazzling success compared with the performance of Estonia's old colonial master, Russia. . . . Officially, GDP is expected to grow by 6% this year; but, if you add in unrecorded activity in the private sector real growth may top 10%." (p. 60).

86. See The Economist's article: "New Zealand; Success Story," (July 9, 1994, p. 40).

87. This information has been extracted from: "New Zealand: Economic and Financial Overview," (February 1994, p. 7–10).

88. The data presented in this section has primarily been extracted from: "New Zealand; Economic and Financial Overview," (February 1994). The article: "New Zealand; Success Story," (The Economist, July 9th, 1994). And the article: "The New Zealand Experiment," (The Wall Street Journal, July 21st, 1994).

89. Trade across these two nations flourished since the Australia New Zealand Closer Economic Relations Trade Agreement (CER) was signed in 1983. The main objective of the agreement was to join the two countries in a free trade zone area by 1995. Furthermore, the two nations opened up the aviation industry to competition from Australasian airlines in 1992.

90. Additionally, New Zealand is a member of the Asian Pacific Economic Cooperation group, which promotes regional trade and economic integration.

91. New Zealand's geographic distribution of exports by countries include more than 20 countries. These are in order of importance: Australia, Japan, United States, England, South Korea, Taiwan, Germany, Hong Kong, Malaysia, China, Canada, Singapore, and other European nations.

92. We should point out that this trend could turn around rapidly, since FDI figures are very volatile and can be distorted by the single acquisition of one firm

93. Our hypotheses is that a small open economy like New Zealand, as compared to a larger counterpart such as Australia, is more likely to manage economic variables in such a way to make its currency undervalued, thus gaining competitiveness in its export related industries.

94. The behavior of the exchange rate under the floating system has been somewhat unpredictable, with respect to the US-NZ dollar exchange going from 49.8 cents in 1985, up to 65.5 cents in 1988, down to 57.5 in 1991, and back up to 63.5 cents in 1995. Even though the exchange rate has fluctuated up and down in the last decade, the fluctuation has not been very dramatic given both the extreme volatility of major currencies through this period and huge structural changes taking place domestically.

95. Moreover, monetary policy can be adjusted in response to fundamental pressures on the exchange rate.

96. For further detail see the publication: "New Zealand: Economic and Financial Overview," (February 1994).

97. See article in "The Economist" (July 9th, 1994, p. 40): "New Zealand: Success Story."

98. After the last elections of 1993, the National Party was re-elected with a narrow majority. Four political parties are represented in Parliament: the National Party, the Labor Party, the Alliance Party (formed from five minority groups), and the New Zealand First Party.

99. It should be pointed out that New Zealand has no specific tax incentives for R&D, and accounting for it may not be as sophisticated as in other developed countries.

100. According to the article: "The New Zealand Experiment," in the Wall Street Journal (July 21, 1994), there is already a plan to reduce the total public debt to around 30% of GDP by 1997.

101. New Zealand, a small nation, will be compared to the large nation of Australia in the statistical analysis, since both countries have similar characteristics.

102. The hypothesis that the means of the two countries of observations are equal cannot be rejected. The lack of data and the insufficient number of degrees of freedom may be an explanation for the insignificance of the statistical results.

103. New Zealand's inflation can be attributed in great part to structural problems, similar to Portugal and Greece's inflationary difficulties in the European Union.

104. The lack of data during the late 1980's, while all the major changes were occurring, probably distorted the results.

105. Once again, the lack of data for the late 1980's probably misrepresented the outcome.

106. The lack of data did not appear to distort the results of this proposition. Akoorie, Michelle, "The Investment Development Cycle:

The Case of New Zealand," *Paper presented on Foreign Direct Investment, Economic Structure and Governments*(Forthcoming), The United Nations University & Erasmus Universiteit, Rotterdam, Dec 15–16, 1994.

# Bibliography


Alesina, Alberto and Spolaore, Enrico. 1995. "On the Number and Size of Nations," National Bureau of Economic Research Cambridge, Mass.: Working Paper No. 5050.

Angresano, James. 1992. *Comparative Economics*, Englewood Cliffs, N.J.: Prentice Hall, Inc.

Balassa, Bela. 1978. "Exports and Economic Growth," *Journal of Development Economics*, Vol. 5: 181–189.

Becker, Gary. 1990. "Actually, Small-Fry Nations Can Do Just Fine," *Business Week*, Oct. 1: 20.

———. 1994."Why so Many Mice Roaring," *Busines Week*, Nov. 7: 20.

Bellak, Christian. 1993. "Foreign Direct Investment from Small States and European Integration: Micro and Macro evidence from Austria," in V.C. Simoes, ed., *International Business and Europe after 1992: Proceedings of the 19th Conference of EIBA*, Vol. 2, Lisboa: CEDE: 237–261.

Bellak, Christian and Luostarinen, Reijo. 1994. *Foreign Direct Investment of Small Open Economies: Case of Austria and Finland*, Helsinki, Finland: HSE Press.

Blondal, Gisli. 1986. *Fiscal Policy in the Smaller Industrial Countries,1972–1982*, Washington, D.C., IMF.

Blundell-Wignall, Adrian and Gregory, Robert G. 1990. "Exchange Rate Policy in Advanced Commodity-Exporting Countries: Australia and New Zealand," in V. Argy and P. De Grauwe ed., *Choosing an Exchange Rate Regime; the Challenge for Smaller Industrial Countries*, Washington, D.C., IMF: 224–271.

Boltho, Andrea. 1982. *The European Economy: Growth and Crisis*, New York: Oxford University Press.

Boyd, Alastair. 1988. *The Essence of Catalonia*, London: Andre Deutsch.

Butter, Anton J. 1985. *An Introduction to Mini-Economics*, Amsterdam, The Netherlands: B.R. Gruner Publishing Co.: 21–64.

Caravelis, Georges. 1994. *European Monetary Union*, Aldershot, Great Britain: Athenaeum Press Ltd.

Castello, Sergio A. and Terutomo Ozawa. 1994. "Globalization of Small Economies as a Strategy Behavior," *Paper presented at the 1994 annual meetings of the Association of International Trade and Finance*, The University of Reading, U.K., July 14–16: 71–85.

Chenery, Hollis B. and Taylor, Lance. 1968. "Development Patterns: Among Countries and Over Time," *The Review of Economics and Statistics*, Vol. L, No. 4: 391–416.

Chow, Peter C.Y. 1987. "Causality Between Export Growth and Industrial Development," *Journal of Development Economics*, Vol. 26: 55–63.

Clark, Barry S. 1991. *Political Economy: A Comparative Approach*, New York: Praeger Publisher.

Collignon, Stefan, Bofinger, Peter, Johnson, Christopher and de Maigret Bertrand. 1994. *Europe's Monetary Future*, Great Britain: Fairleigh Dickinson University Press.

De Grauwe, Paul & Wim Vanhaverbeke. 1990. "Exchange Rate Experiences of Small EMS Countries: Belgium, Denmark, and The Netherlands," in V. Argy and P. De Grauwe ed., *Choosing and Exchange Rate Regime: The Challenge for Smaller Industrial Countries*, Washington, D.C.,IMF: 135–155.

Demas, William G. 1965. *The Economics of Development in SmallCountries*, Montreal, Canada: McGill University Press: 39–91.

Dervis, Kemal, De Melo, Jaime and Robinson, Sherman. 1982. *General Equilibrium Models for Development Policy*, New York: Cambridge University Press.

Dodaro, Santo. 1991. "Comparative Advantage, Trade and Growth: Export-Led Growth Revisited," *World Development*, Vol. 19, No. 9: 1153–1165.

Dollar, David. 1992. "Outward Oriented Developing Economies Really Do Grow More Rapidly: Evidence from 95 LDCs, 1976–1985,"

*Economic Development and Cultural Change*, Vol. 40, No. 3: 523–544.

———. 1991. "Outward Orientation and Growth: An Empirical Study Using a Price-Based Measure of Openness," *Background Paper for the 1991 WDR*: 1–36.

Dommen, Edward and Hein, Philippe. 1985. *States, Microstates and Islands*, Beckenham, Great Britain: Croom Helm Ltd.: 152–184.

Dunning, John H. 1992. "The Global Economy, Domestic Governance, Strategies and Transnational Corporations: Interactions and Policy Implications," *Transnational Corporations*, Vol. 1, No. 3, December: 7–45.

———. 1982. "The Eclectic Theory of the Multinational Enterprise," in A.M. Rugman, ed., *New Theories of theMultinational Enterprise*, London, England: Croom Helm Ltd.

———. 1981. "Explaining the International Direct Investment Position of Countries: Towards a Dynamic or Developmental Approach," *Weltwirtschaftliches Archiv*, 11, 1: 30–64.

El-Agraa, Ali M. 1982. *International Economic Integration*, New York: St. Martin's Press.

Esfahani, Hadi Salehi. 1991. "Exports, Imports and Economic Growth in Semi-Industrialized Countries," *Journal of Development Economics*, Vol. 35: 93–116.

Gayle, Dennis. 1986. *The Small Developing State: ComparingEconomies in Costa Rica, Singapore, and Jamaica*, Brookfield, Vermont: Gower Publishing Co.

Grant, Wyn. 1985. *The Political Economy of Corporatism*, New York: St. Martin's Press.

Griffiths, William, Hill, R. Carter and Judge, George. 1993. *Learning and Practicing Econometrics*, New York: John Wiley & Sons, Inc.: 571–579.

Grossman, Gene M. and Helpman, Elhanan. 1994. "Endogenous Innovation in the Theory of Growth," *Journal of Economic Perspectives*, Vol. 8, Number, 1, Winter: 23–44.

———. 1991. *Innovation and Growth in the Global Economy*, Cambridge, Mass.: MIT Press.

Helpman, Elhanan. 1992. "Endogeneous Macroeconomic Growth Theory," *National Bureau of Economic Research*, Cambridge, Mass.: Working Paper Reprint No. 1773.

Henley, Andrew and Tsakalotos, Euclid. 1993. *Corporatism andEconomic Performance*, Cambridge, Great Britain: Edward Elgar Publishing Limited.

Hirsch, Seen and Thomsen, Steen. 1993. "Internationalization of Small Country Industrial Firms: A Comparative Study of Denmark and Israel," *Proceedings of the 19th Annual Conference of EIBA*, Vol. 2, December 1993, Lisboa, Portugal: 237–261.

Horsman, George. 1988. *Inflation in the Twentieth Century*, New York: St. Martin's Press.

Hutchison, Michael. 1995. *Central Bank Credibility and Disinflation in New Zealand*, Federal Reserve Bank of San Francisco Weekly Letter, Nu. 95–06, February 10.

IMF. 1991–1992. *International Financial Statistics*, Washington, D.C., IMF.

IMD. 1993. *The World Competitiveness Report*, Lausanne, Switzerland: IMD Publication, 13th Edition.

Jacobs, Jake. 1984. *Cities and the Wealth of Nations: Principles of Economic Life*, New York: Random House.

Jalan, Bimal. 1982. *Problems and Policies in Small Economies*, New York: St. Martin's Press: 17–47 and 143–184.

Johnson, Bjorn. 1988. "An Institutional Approach to the Small Country Problem," in C. Freeman & B.A. Lundvall, ed., *Small Countries Facing the Technological Revolution*, London, England: Pinter Publishers.

Johnston, Hank. 1991. *Tales of Nationalism*, New Brunswick: Rutgers University Press.

Jones, Eric L. 1987. *The European Miracle*, New York: Cambridge University Press.

Kaminarides, John, Briguglio, Lino and Hoogendonk, Henk N. 1989. *The Economic Development of Small Countries: Problems, Strategies, and Policies*, Delft, The Netherlands: Eburon Publishers.

Killick, Tony. 1993. *The Adaptive Economy: Adjustment Policies in Small, Low Income Countries*, Washington, D.C.: The World Bank.

Kindleberger, Charles. 1984. *Multinational Excursions*, Cambridge, Mass.: MIT Press.

Kohli, Inderjit and Singh, Nirvikar. 1989. "Exports and Growth," *Journal of Development Economics*, Vol. 30: 391–400.

Kohr, Leopold. 1977. *The Overdeveloped Nations: the Diseconomies of Scale*, New York: Schocken Books.

———. 1973. *Development without Aid*, Swansea: Christopher Davies Publishers Ltd.

———. 1957. *The Breakdown of Nations*, New York: Routledge and Kegan Paul.

Krugman, Paul R. 1991. *Geography and Trade*, Leuven, Belgium and Cambridge, Mass.: University Press and the MIT Press.

———. 1990. *Rethinking International Trade*, Cambridge, Mass.: MIT Press.

———. 1987. "Pricing to Market When the Exchange Rate Changes," in S.W. Arndt and J.D. Richardson, ed., *Real Financial Linkages Among Open Economies*, Cambridge, Mass.: MIT Press: 49–70.

Kugler, Peter. 1991. "Growth, Exports and Cointegration: An Empirical Investigation," *Weltwirtschaftliches Archiv*, b. 127 h. 1: 73–82.

Kuznets, Simon. 1960. "Economic Growth of Small Nations," In E.A.G. Robinson, ed., *The Economic Consequences of the Size of Nations*, New York: St. Martin's Press: 14–32.

Lachman, Ludwig M. 1970. *The Legacy of Max Weber*, London, England: Heinemann.

Laking, George R. 1963. *The Economic Development of New Zealand and the Impact of the European Economic Community*, New Jersey: Princeton University Press.

Lattimore, Ralph. 1987. "Economic Adjustment in New Zealand: A Developed Country Case Study of Policies and Problems," in Sir Frank Holmes ed., *Economic Adjustment: policies and Problems*, Washington, D.C., IMF: 34–84.

Lleonart, Pere. 1992. *Catalonia: a Land, an Economy*, Barcelona, Spain: Generalitat de Catalunya, and Official Chamber of Commerce, Industry, and Navigation of Barcelona.

Naisbitt, John. 1994. *The Global Paradox*, New York: William Morrow and Co. Inc.

New Zealand Debt Management Office. 1994. *New Zealand: Economic and Financial Overview*, Wellington, New Zealand: The Treasury, February.

Niehans, Jurg. 1977. "Benefits of Multinational Firms for Small Parent Economy: The Case of Switzerland," in Tamir Agmon and Charles Kindleberger, eds., *Multinationals from SmallCountries*, Cambridge, Mass.: MIT Press: 1–39.

North, Douglass C. 1981. *Structure and Change in Economic History*, New York: W.W. Norton & Company, Inc.

OECD, 1983–1989. *Economic Surveys: New Zealand*, Paris, France: OECD publication.

Olson, Mancur. 1982. *The Rise and Decline of Nations*, New Haven & London: Yale University Press.

Ozawa, Terutomo. 1994. "Exploring the Asian Economic Miracle: Politics, Economics, Society, Culture, and History—A Review Article," *The Journal of Asian Studies 53*, No. 1, Feb: 124–131.

———. 1992. "Foreign Direct Investment and Economic Growth," *Transnational Corporations*, Vol. 1, No. 1: 27–54.

———. 1987. "Can the Market alone Manage Structural Upgrading? A Challenge Posed by Economic Interdependence," In John Dunning & M. Usui, ed., *Structural Change, Economic Interdependence and World Development*, London: Macmillan Press.

Persaud, Brian. 1989. "Small States: Economic Problems and Prospects," In Kaminarides, Briguglio and Hoogendonk, ed., *The Economic Development of Small Countries*, Delft, The Netherlands: Eburon Publishers: 15–29.

Plischke, Elmer. 1977. *Microstates in World Affairs*, Washington, D.C: American Enterprise Institute for Public Policy Research.

Polanyi, Karl. 1957. *The Great Transformation*, Boston, Mass: Beacon Press.

Prachowny, Martin F.J. 1984. *Macroeconomic Analysis for Small Open Economies*, New York: Oxford University Press.

Prebble, Mark. 1994. *New Zealand: the Turnaround Economy*, London, England: IOD, The Director Publications Ltd.

Puig i Bastard, Pere. 1990. *Atlas Comercial de Catalunya*, Barcelona, Spain: Official Chamber of Commerce, Industry, and Navigation.

Pyne, Lindsay. 1992. "Opportunities in the Market," in the Collection of Papers of the New Zealand Investment Conference, ed., *An Investment for the Future*, Auckland, New Zealand: NZ Investment Conference Publication.

Rapaport, Jacques, Muteba, Ernest and Therattil, Joseph J. 1971. *Small States and Territories; Status and Problems*, New York: Arno Press.

Read, Jan. 1978. *The Catalans*, London & Boston: Faber & Faber.

Robinson, E.A.G. 1960. *The Economic Consequences of the Size of Nations*, New York: St. Martin's Press.

Romer, Paul M. 1990. "Endogeneous Technological Change," *The Journal of Political Economy*, Vol. 98: S71–S102.

———. 1986. "Increasing Returns and Long Run Growth," *TheJournal of Political Economy*, Vol. 94: 1002–1037.

Rosenberg, Jerry. 1994. "Globalization of Regional Economic Integration: Applying the European Union Model," *Paperpresented at the 1994 annual meetings of the Association of International Trade and Finance*, the University of Reading, U.K., July 14–16.

Rostow, W.W. 1971. *The Stages of Economic Growth*, New York: Cambridge University Press.

Sala-i-Martin, Xavier. 1990. *Lecture Notes on Economic Growth*, Cambridge Mass.: NBER, Working Papers No. 3563 & 3564.

Sarkar, Prabirjit and Singer, H.W. 1991. "Manufactured Exports of Developing Countries and their Terms of Trade Since 1965," *World Development*, Vol. 19, No. 4: 333–340.

Schmitter, Philippe C. 1981. "Interest Intermediation and Regime Governability in Contemporary Western Europe and North America," In S. Berger, ed., *Organizing Interests in Western Europe*, England: Edward Elgar Publishing Ltd.: 285–327.

Schou, August and Brundtland, Arne Olav. 1971. *Small States in International Relations*, Stockholm, Sweden: Almquist & Wiksell.

Schumacher, Ernst F. 1973. *Small is Beautiful*, New York: Harper & Row Publishers.

Schumpeter, Joseph. 1934. *The Theory of Economic Development*, Cambridge, Mass.: Harvard University Press.

Senjur, Marjan. 1992. "The Viability of Economic Development of a Small State Separating from a Larger One,". *Development & International Cooperation*, Vol. VIII, No. 14–15, June-Dec: 5–22.

Sephton, Peter S. 1989. "Causality Between Export Growth and Industrial Development," *Journal of Development Economics*, Vol. 31: 413–415.

Sherwin, Murray. 1991. "Capital Market Liberalization: The New Zealand Experience," in S. Hanke and A. Walters ed., *Capital Markets and Development*, San Francisco, California: Institute for Contemporary Studies Press: 209–240.

Smith, Adam. 1976. *An Inquiry into the Nature and Causes of the Wealth of Nations*, London: Methuen & Co. Ltd., as reproduced by E. Cannan (1904).

Sobrer, Josep M. 1992. *Catalonia, a Self-Portrait*, Bloomington & Indianapolis: Indiana University Press.

Solow, Robert M. 1956. "A Contribution to the Theory of Economic Growth," *Quarterly Journal of Economics*, 70:65–94.

———. 1957. "Technical Change and the Aggregate Production Function," *Review of Economic Statistics*, 31: 312–320.

———. 1994. "Perspectives on Growth Theory," *Journal ofEconomic Perspectives*, Vol. 8, No. 1, Winter: 45–54.

Streeten, Paul. 1993. "The Special Problems of Small Nations," *World Development*, Vol. 21, No. 2: 197–202.

Summers, Robert and Heston, Alan. 1988. "The Penn World Tables (Mark 5): An Expanded Set of International Comparisons, 1950–88," *Quarterly Journal of Economics*, 105 (2): 327–368.

Throop, Adrian W. 1994. *The Real Effects of Exchange Rates*, Federal Reserve Bank of San Francisco Weekly Letter, Nu. 94–03, January 21.

Thurow, Lester. 1992. *Head to Head*, New York: William Morrow and Company, Inc.

TRADENZ. 1993–1994. *Stretching for Growth: Building an Export Strategy for New Zealand*, Wellington, New Zealand: a New Zealand Trade Development Board Publication.

UNCTAD. 1994. *World Investment Report: Transnational Corporations*, New York, Geneva: U.N. Publication.

Williamson, Peter, J. 1989. *Corporatism in Perspective*, London, England: SAGE Publications Ltd.

Womack, James P., Jones, Daniel T. and Roos, Daniel. 1990. *The Machine that Changed the World*, New York: Macmillan.

Wood, John, H. 1992. "Monetary Policy in a Small Open Economy: The Case of Singapore," *Economic Review: Federal Reserve Bank of Dallas*, 2nd Quarter: 25–41.

World Bank. 1993. *The East Asian Miracle*, New York: Oxford University Press.

———. 1994. *World Development Report*, Baltimore, Maryland: The John Hopkins University.

# Index

For Product Safety Concerns and Information please contact our EU
representative GPSR@taylorandfrancis.com
Taylor & Francis Verlag GmbH, Kaufingerstraße 24, 80331 München, Germany

www.ingramcontent.com/pod-product-compliance
Lightning Source LLC
LaVergne TN
LVHW021036011026
849160LV00009BA/667

* 9 7 8 1 1 3 8 9 7 5 2 8 6 *